MW00583609

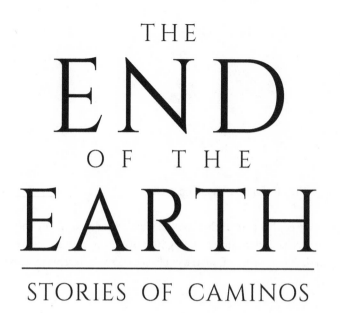

THE
END
OF THE
EARTH
STORIES OF CAMINOS

DR. GUYLENE GIGI TREE

WRITERS REPUBLIC L.L.C.
515 Summit Ave. Unit R1
Union City, NJ 07087, USA

Website: *www.writersrepublic.com*
Hotline: *1-877-656-6838*
Email: *info@writersrepublic.com*

Ordering Information:
Quantity sales. Special discounts are available on quantity purchases by corporations, associations, and others. For details, contact the publisher at the address above.

Library of Congress Control Number: 2020938590
ISBN-13:   978-1-64620-367-3   [Paperback Edition]
                  978-1-64620-368-0   [Digital Edition]

Rev. date: 05/13/2020

The end of the earth

"Life is either a daring adventure or nothing at all."
~ Helen Keller

PROLOGUE - DEAR READER

I was standing on a cliff overlooking the Atlantic Ocean. Cliffs to my right, cliffs to my left. Right there, at that very point where I stood, was recorded in history as "the end of the earth." The farthest point west on the European continent, a place where it was once presumed, if you sailed out you would fall off the earth.

This story is not of a trip along the famous Camino de Santiago de Compostela, rather a sharing of the culture, food, people, sights and sounds of remarkable journeys on roads that have been traveled upon for a few thousand years by multitudes of pilgrims. It is not a travel journal, rather a collection of stories, experiences, information and sharing of encounters good, bad, funny, sad, profound, eye-opening, well, you get the gist. You may read the stories in order or look for a title that captures your fancy and jump in. Some stories play off others but can also be enjoyed independently. Think of this book as a buffet with no rules. Please enjoy. Buen Camino

PARIS IN JUNE

Why do people get all wobbly legged when you say the word "Paris?" I mean, look at this airport! Is this really something that dreams are made of? There's mom over there with the three kids in tow, babe in arms, toddler screaming with a nose full of snot, older brother wishing he could be anywhere but here attached to this tangle of calamity. And dad? Where's dad? Oh, there he is, pushing the luggage cart, bubble wrap encrusted baby stroller, duffle bags, suitcases, diaper bags,  cartoon logo children's bag falling, falling, falling gone and taking out two bags on the way down. Crash, burn, yard sale as one split open spilling out a myriad of lotions, underclothing, flip flops and Hawaiian flowered shirts.

Pan right and we observe the oh so blond oh so blue-eyed group of young Scandinavian girls with backpacks engaging in nonstop cackle in their native tongue, all the young boys looking google eyed at the gaggle. In their dreams? Well, one never knows. It is, after all, summer in Paris.

I love watching people. If there was such thing as a job with the description "people watcher," I would be the absolute best in the industry. But, enough about that. So, why am I here in the Paris airport, among all the glitter and flash of this newly renovated hub of travel? I am beginning an adventure that had its initial genesis in my deep imagination years ago and has taken me through 65 years of living to achieve the dream. I am walking the Camino de Santiago de Compostela.

After months of careful planning, packing, checking weight, unpacking, packing, checking weight, I finally had my backpack filled with everything I would need for the 1,000 plus kilometer trek down to a mere 8 pounds without water. The water, which would be added later, would top my pack to just under 10 pounds. Perfect for my 5 feet almost one inch, 80-pound soaking wet body. At the present I was looking out the window onto the tarmac where my plane awaited, not in one of those handy dandy swing out hook on people loaders, but out in the rain with a set of roll-up stairs being pushed up to the open door. And look at that luggage bin over-stuffed with baggage. Was that my backpack on top getting soaked in the deluge from the sky. Geez…no…there is a roll up tarp. Can someone please just cover up the bin? On the bottom of the cart are stacked all those impenetrable plastic roll on wheels suitcases of plastic titanium or similar man-fabricated materials. Why couldn't those be on top.

---※ **2** ※---

BIARRITZ -GETTING TO SAINT JEAN PIED du PORT

European air travel is the complete antithesis of safety-oriented, gender-neutral, elastic-smile, self- shielded type of ride that we have become obsessed about in the US. In Europe it is "there's the plane, grab your stuff and here we go" attitude. Seated in the small, overstuffed cabin of the only airline servicing the small seaside port of Biarritz, I am surrounded by a mélange of humanity, seemingly only slightly outnumbered by the oversized suitcases each individual has packed onto their laps, in the isles, hanging out of the overflowing above head bins. We even have three dogs of nondescript breed categories being adoringly caressed by the owner in an attempt to distract them from attacking the other animals, human and non-human alike. Children run the aisles oblivious of the adult-initiated attempts to quiet them or at least partially contain them.

After a little over one hour of in-flight pandemonium the little plane makes a big half circle which initiates the beginning of descent as well as the awakening of all those who had been successful in their attempts at sleep. Rapid descent, ear-popping, stomach flipping, seemingly frozen moment in time and bump, bump, ba-bump bump, and we are down. The passengers erupt into spontaneous applause. Really?

Down on the tarmac, roll out the stair's contraption, and outcome all sorts of excited, exhausted, elated, euphoric, and just plain ol' enthusiastic mix of humanity all thankful to be back on terra firma. That is, at least I am. Don't know about all the others. However, all I can think of is retrieving my wet backpack so I can assess the damage.

Ka thunk, ka thunk, ka thunk and the conveyer belt of infinity begins its slow acceleration into the metronomic dumping of belongings that people have deemed necessary for their journey. One circuit and, oh lucky me, there it sits in all its glory. One baby blue backpack with two patches. The first is the small round stylized scallop shell with its 9 points, yellow for the shell on a blue background. This is the symbol of the Camino, the route marker, the one which I would become awfully familiar with as I searched for them along the way for they indicated that I was still on the trail. The second patch is a white and blue Megan David or Star of David. Yes, I am Jewish…Jewish by birth and Jewish by religion. So why you might ask is a religious Jew doing a Catholic Pilgrimage? That my friend is a story for later. First, we must get the backpack.

Yes, it is wet, not bad but definitely wet. I will hopefully be able to pull everything out tonight and dry all items that are wet, then repack for the first day of my Camino which begins tomorrow. But for now, it is still raining, and I need to find a bus, then a train. This great backpack has a wonderful rain cover that magically pulls out of the bottom. I think this is such a smart, clever, and unique item until I see that everyone in the airport with a backpack has the identical rain gizmo. Get the pack covered, get the person covered, get the pack on, and off we go.

First on the agenda is finding the bus that will take me from the Biarritz airport to the Bayonne Rail Station where I can get the train to Saint Jean Pied du Port. This village, on the east side of the French Pyrenees, is the beginning point for the Camino Frances, or the historical route

THE END OF THE EARTH

that pilgrims from France used to take back in the first century. I am an experienced traveler and have learned that when I pull into a new town the first thing I do is get a map. Therefore, I head to the TI (tourist information) and grab one. As I do so I ask for directions to the bus that will take me to the train station in Bayonne. My French is actually fairly good, so all this conversation is feeling pretty natural.

I'm back in travel mode, a state of being that I just love. However, (and when things are going too well there is always a however), the map is not a beautiful color-coded tourist map, but a hand drawn, poor quality, photocopy map showing alternative directions to the bus stop since there is major construction going on. OK, this can't be too bad. After all, this is a small town. The bus stop must be visible from the exit to the airport. I mean, they can't hide a bus stop. Right?

I head out in the rain with map in hand trying to decipher the hieroglyphics which are becoming wet and smudged. According to the map, the bus should be here. Nope. But there are two other backpackers seemingly in the same situation. I approach the two ladies asking if they are looking for the bus to Bayonne. In Italian they inform me that they are also looking for the bus…at least that is what I think they are saying. After a few words it turns out that they do not speak any English but speak a little French so that is the language we use. They have the same map as I have and have had no better luck in deciphering it. We decide that the main road going in a north-south direction in front of the airport must be a major road and therefore busses must travel it. You see, the construction zone has taken out about a good half mile of this road directly in front of the airport obliterating any possibility of a bus stop. Therefore, our best bet is to either travel north above the construction or south below the construction. The three of us opt for south since that is the direction of the main part of Biarritz. Off we go putting the maps in the first trash bin we see. And, by the way, it is still raining.

After about a 4- or 5-kilometer walk, we finally come upon a bus stop. Eureka! Now then, just what bus stop we have no idea. It says the number line in bold letters on the sign post but inside the small shelter the route and specifics are weatherworn to just a pasty off-white layer of what seem to be 10 or 15 various historical maps of this route, none of which have legible printing. So, we all decide to wait for the next bus and ask where it is going.

Now that we are all stopped and somewhat sheltered from the rain, we have an opportunity to visit and share information about each other. My two Italian friends are Paola and Claudetta from Milano. They are on a two-week holiday and plan to begin in Saint Jean Pied du Port and just see how far they get. No plans and no hurry. They have done other routes before including the last 100 kilometers of this route, from Sarria to Santiago and the Norte, the route that follows the north coastline of Spain. This will be their first time going over the Pyrenees. They are both heavy smokers and rapidly go through a half dozen of the Italian version of the French Gauloise. My immediate thoughts are how can they be such heavy smokers and be planning on embarking upon a trek up, over and down the Pyrenees, a climb which is not by any means a cakewalk. This is serious climbing. And with a backpack? Each of their individual backpacks weigh at least twice what mine does. Yes, they are big ladies but still… Oh well, it seems they know what they are doing.

We have a lovely visit learning details of each other obtainable through our limited fluency in French. Through my Google Translate app I was able to compose sentences in English and translate them into Italian. They in turn did the same. Interesting way to communicate. Thirty minutes or so later and a bus arrives. Lo and behold, it says "Gare" on it which means train station. Great. We hand the driver our two euro and hop on. We are headed to the train station to catch our 1:30 train, or are we, maybe? I mentally calculate that this trip should take about 15 minutes. In less than 5 minutes we arrive at a train station. This can't be the correct one. Nope, it isn't. We are at the Biarritz Gare not the Bayonne Gare. OK, not a problem. They must have a transfer bus. Where is the TI? Bus schedule in hand and real map this time we all make it to the proper bus and problem solved. Aaahhhh.

3

SAINT JEAN PIED
du PORT

I have a four-day two country rail pass and a reservation, so I am good to go. My Italian friends do not. The ticket office is on lunch break and will not open until 4:00 PM. The train leaves at 1:30. I say goodbye to my new travel friends and we all agree that we will probably see each other somewhere along the Camino. Arrivederci! Ciao.

This train is honestly the shortest train I have ever seen. It is one main engine car and two passenger cars with half of one designated for first class. I hop on, find a seat, and hope the train will start soon so the heater will come on. I am wet and cold. I promptly take off all my wet stuff and spread it out along the heater vent area below the window. I am not a newbie to European train travel. Time to go online with my phone and do some posts to Facebook. Finding the local SCNF (French Train) network I log on and upload.

As I was one of the first people to get on the train I now get to "people watch" as all my fellow Camino walkers find their seats and take off their wet stuff. It is an interesting mix of people. We have the group of 4 college students on summer holiday from a Catholic private college on the East coast. Their excitement is uncontrollable. Extremely cute. Their backpacks are out of control. Huge. Then we have the two older women, easily in their upper 70's, from either Belgium or northern France from their accent. Across the way we have the young married couple from Australia. She is a veterinarian in a small animal practice, and he is in investing of some sort. They are on a six-week trip, four weeks on the Camino and two weeks visiting relatives in England. Up front are two drop dead gorgeous male specimens in their early 20's from Norway. They are enjoying the attention from the Catholic college girls. All these diverse people all united in one common factor; we are all going to walk the Camino de Santiago de Compostela.

So why would a person choose to undertake this journey? It is over 500 miles of walking hills, mountains, valleys, lowlands, highlands, big cities, small villages, streams, rivers, rain, heat, bugs, blisters, muscle aches, tendon abuse, sometimes even stomach abuse. I know what my reasons are. Learning of the reasons of others is all part of the Camino experience, the Lessons of the Camino.

After about a 30-minute ride our little train pulls into the tiny train station of Saint Jean Pied du Port. All 30 or so pilgrims pile out of the two cars and into the tiny building where we grab a map and head out the front door for the two-block walk to the old city. Oh, my goodness, what a lovely place! This cute little village, built outside of the citadel with one main street encircled with the sandstone walls, just begs to be investigated. Cute little shops selling everything from essential items for pilgrims to fresh sweets to soaps and spices. But, there will be time later. First on my agenda is to locate my Airbnb, check in, unload, and unpack my pack then get a warm shower.

ACCOMMODATIONS OF THE CAMINOS

No matter your finances, likes, dislikes, perceived needs, desired facilities, your requirements can be met in the accommodations available on all the Caminos. Perhaps not when you need them, or think you need them, but they are there...somewhere. The focus of this info-story is to emphasize the point that what you think you need may not be what in reality you need. Be flexible and allow the Camino to direct you. If you do not have any expectations, you will not be disappointed.

The following information briefly details the various types of accommodations available and what they provide.

ALBERGES / REFUGIOS / HOSTELS -by far the most numerous types of accommodations on the Caminos are these. They all provide some type of bed, typically bunk beds in a common room but some have private or semi-private rooms. Often a communal pilgrim meal is offered at the facility. Some have an open kitchen where you can make your own dinner. They typically open in the mid-afternoon, lock the doors at 10 or 11 and expect you out by 8 in the morning. They do not take reservations and rent beds on a first come first served basis. They have communal shower and toilet facilities but are not always segregated. You usually must provide your own sleeping bag. These facilities are only open for pilgrims and you must present you pilgrim passport to rent a space for the night. No "double dipping" or two nights allowed. One night maximum. Check in after 3 PM and out by 8 AM. This is no frills basic lodging at an inexpensive price.

GUEST HOUSES / PENSIONES -these are typically privately owned by families as a business. Most rooms have a private bath but some share. Often the pensiones will offer various types of accommodation plans such as full board which includes breakfast, lunch and dinner, or half board including two of the three meals. One can also opt for the room only plan.

HOTEL -in the larger Camino towns and cities, you will find a large selection of hotels ranging from 3-star to 4-and 5-star ratings. The most well-known hotels in Spain are the Paradores. These are luxury hotels that belong to the state-owned company *Paradores Spain*. They are typically historic buildings such as castles and monasteries and have been completely restored with all modern conveniences while keeping the old character.

HOW MANY CAMINOS
ARE THERE?

Traditionally the Camino started from your front door. So, the number of pilgrims, the number of front doors, that is how many Caminos there are. As pilgrims' walks brought them closer to Spain, the various trails would merge becoming wider, more populated and providing more services to the travelers. On the more traveled paths, churches, monasteries, and other religious structures were erected affording the pilgrims a place for the night. These structures were placed approximately one day walking apart from each other. They

allowed the traveler the ability to hop-scotch across Spain staying each night at a facility that would give them a bed and a meal. Around these structures blossomed villages providing an ever-increasing amount of services to the pilgrims, ultimately building the infrastructure of modern Spain.

I have completed two Caminos over two years which I will share stories of later in this book. My first year was the Camino Frances, the most popular Camino which begins in Saint Jean Pied du Port. I walked this one all the way to Santiago de Compostela, 790 kilometers, then on to Finisterre, an additional 87 kilometers, and dipped my toes in the Atlantic. This journey addicted me to this type of travel and the next year I did the Celtic Camino.

Many of the roads in Spain were traveled by persons other than pilgrims a long time before there was such a thing as Christianity. The Celts held sacred various points in Galicia as ritual sites and would journey there for ceremonial customs. One such place is the *Cruz de Ferro* or Iron Cross. Located between the villages of Rabanal del Camino and Ponferrada, it was originally used by the Celts, then by the Romans as a territory boundary marker, then finally by the Christians who put a cross atop the wooden pole. This Celtic Camino for me began in Dublin, Ireland walking about 100 km then flying to Madrid to continue to Santiago, a distance of 600 kilometers.

My next Camino which will be my third, and longest Camino will be Via de la Plata and Camino Sanabres. This Camino begins in Sevilla and travels 974 kilometers to Santiago approaching from the south. This route was originally a Roman road with the primary function of transportation of silver from the north to the south, hence the name Via de la Plata or the Silver Route. At the writing of this book, my plane ticket is for June. Coved 19 is delaying that trip but I will make it, just don't know when. Sounds like a second book is in the future; the Camino post Coved 19.

6

MY ALL-TIME MOST EXHAUSTING DAY

I live, work, and play at altitude. As an avid skier and a working Ski Patroller, hard work at altitude is not a problem. As I studied my maps, learned of the start at 200 meters elevation, climbing to 1,400 meters, then back to 900 meters over a distance of 24 kilometers, I knew it would be a long and hard day, but doable. I was up for the challenge. After a lovely stay at a Pension in Saint Jean Pied du Port, up before the sun to get an early start, I began the Camino through the medieval village and on to the tarmac road leading up over the Pyrenees. What a beautiful way to spend day one on the Camino Frances!

As I watched the sun share its light across rolling green hills with sheep, horses, and cows, I had to remind myself this was real. Scattered along the way were picturesque cottages and barns, farmland luscious pastureland and even some deer. As I gained elevation the land changed becoming much less populated by structures but more populated by rocks and dirt. Then, a few clouds. More clouds…mist…rain. Time to stop and pull out the rain cover for my pack and put on my rain jacket. The temperature was warm, so I had on shorts. No big deal. If my legs get wet, they will dry. All adjusted for the rain and I was off again.

Before I continue in this exciting narration, let me say a word or two about my stature. I am petite. No, really petite. Five feet and a scooch, 80 pounds soaking wet. But, I have long legs for my height resulting in a stride which most would describe as fast. With the drizzle turning into a goose-drowner rain, I used my fastest stride to make tracks. From my phone app I knew that there was an Albergue in Orisson just a few kilometers up the trail. There I could dry out a bit and wait for the storm to pass or, if necessary, just stop for the night. After all, I was on no timetable.

The Refuge Orison, just outside the village of Hunto, was lovely. Nice warm fire with scattered tables and seating made for a perfect spot for a coffee con leche and croissant. But, no available beds at the Inn. So, bundle back up and keep trekking. Fortunately, the rainstorm had passed but the clouds were still playing peek-a-boo with the sun.

The trail was now becoming very steep with switchbacks and ridge walks and big rocks to navigate. The grassy dirt path was a slippery, boot sucking, unstable, boggy mess. I was passing hikers who had obviously succumbed to the muddy monster and were covered in the grey goo. I just hoped that would not become my fate.

Not only was the grey goo difficult to walk in, the terrain made for a turtle speed pace. The goo was creeping up my hiking boots, past my socks and halfway up my legs when I crested the summit. My feeling of elation was so great that I was not taking in the whole picture. Coming up the goo was bad. Now I had to go down the goo! I was only 18 kilometers into the route with 6 more to go and the sun was in the subtle declaration of impending darkness. I had begun my day at 5:30 AM and it was closing in on 4:30 PM. My cadence was "step, slog, step, slog, slip, woops, step, slog.

Finally, 5:30 PM I round the hill and see the gorgeous, stone edifice. Wow! Albergue de Peregrinos Roncasvalles, an amazing, huge, old edifice outside but quite modern inside, is finally a reality. As I stumble inside the kindest older gentleman welcomes this tired pilgrim with a smile and friendly gesture for me to sit down. He helps me take my pack off and gives me the paperwork to fill out letting me know that there is no hurry. I may rest until I have the strength to hold the pen. I am so wasted.

After filling out the paperwork, getting my pilgrim passport stamped, he picks up my backpack and tells me to follow him and he will show me to my cubical and bunk. We slowly make out way down the halls and enter a huge room with a myriad of cubicles, each with 4 bunk beds. Before entering he helps me to another bench just outside and lets me know that I must take off my boots and place them in the rack. The look on my face must have been one of one "I can't move much less take off my boots." This dear man gets down on his knees and removes my boots for me. He then assists me to my bunk and places my backpack at the foot of the bed and wishes me a good rest.

Totally spent I just collapse on my bed for a bit. It is only 6:30 or so and the pilgrim's meal is served at 7:30 in the huge dining hall. I manage to get myself up, shuffle into the bathroom, clean myself up, crawl into my sleeping bag and I am out. The hardest most exhausting day of my life...but what a wonderful adventure.

7

VILLAMAYOR DE MONJARDIN AND A CATTLE GUARD

The lovely village of Villamayor, located at the foot of the Castle of San Esteban of Deyo, makes for an agreeable overnight stop. The moderate uphill grade coming into the village is like what one reads about in storybooks. The knight in shining armor riding into the hamlet on a white steed coming to rendezvous with his damsel. Oh wait, snap, back to reality. There are cows, dwellings, gardens, a few parked cars. All very quaint.

The castle dates from the 10th century and is not on the tourist route nor is it restored in any fashion. It is genuinely a castle that has been left to the elements for the past 10 centuries and a real find if you like those sorts of things which, I do. You can walk around the outside and see the walls which sit atop a Roman foundation. Apparently, the edifice has been repeatedly rebuilt over the centuries.

The evening included a nice pilgrim's meal with great wine and a single room for a perfect rest after a long day. Early the next morning I was up before the sun as I love to do. Out the door and down the path to rejoin the Camino.

Hitting the Camino before the sun comes up has many positive advantages, very few or no other pilgrims. Positive ones include, no or very few other pilgrims. Quiet solitude with lovely sounds of morning birds and animals. Watching the world awake to a new day as the sun rises. The big negative is that it is dark, the Camino arrows or signs can be missed.

The path out of town was easy to find as it was a very small town. The main road leads in and the continuation of same road led out. Beginning as a single wide road, it soon became a two-lane road, then a divided two-lane road, then a big divided four lane highway with zooming cars and trucks. This can't be the way. I must have missed a turn way back there.

Coming up behind me was the confirmation of my fears in the form of a police car with lights twirling. There Spanish admonishment to me was something like "Lady, what the heck do you think you are doing. This is a freeway and walkers are not allowed. The pilgrim trail is just over there" as they point, and I clearly see it with a couple of pilgrims. The problem is that between this highway and the pilgrim trail there are about 200 yards of trees, steep ravines, and a moderate size river too big to cross. I must turn around and go back.

On the Camino, every step is logged into your "Camino Step Bank" and retracing even one step is more than counterproductive. But retrace my steps I must. Back down the four-lane divided highway, down the smaller four lane highway, down the divided two-lane road, then the regular two-lane road and, on the left, most definitely, was an unmarked path that had to be the Camino. There was no sign but in the dark, even if there had been one, I would not have been able to see it.

The real reason I missed the trail is because it did not look like a trail. It looked like a fenced private pasture with a cattle guard. Oh well, I need to cross. Most cattle guards on the Camino have a small gate off to one side that pilgrims can pass through rather than going across the metal slats. This guard had no such gate. Very carefully I stepped from rail to rail negotiating the intervals over the five-foot framework bridge. Almost across then, woops. My right walking stick missed the rail and continued into the void. The momentum of this action, combined with my top-heavy body and backpack, sent me launching across the "walking stick eating monster" and coming to rest on the asphalt on the other side, face first.

Stars, no kidding, just like in cartoons. I really hit hard. That jelly-like grey matter in my head definitely got a shake. I do have a medical background, so my first action was to triage my situation. What worked and what did not. The injuries were, from least to worst, an abraded right knee and lower leg with imbedded asphalt, a wrist that had been forced beyond the "ouch" limit, and assorted scrapes and bruises. But the worst was the side of my face. The full impact was the right side of my cheek, primarily the zygomatic bone. I had a large avulsion which was producing copious amounts of blood. Facial and scalp wounds often produce a lot of blood, so I was not that worried. My concern was the concussion I had obviously sustained.

Now that I know what's wrong, where the heck am I and where is the next town. From checking my map, I deduced that I had about 5 or 6 miles to get to the next village. Would the village be up at this hour and, more importantly, would they have a first aid facility? Only one option; start walking.

When things like this happen, the lessons of the Camino become so tangible you almost want to yell out to the divine "OK I get it." Out on the Camino the pilgrim is stripped of all but the barest of essentials. You have yourself and the divine to rely upon. No telephone to call 911. No car to transport you to an emergency room. Perhaps not even another person for miles. You reach down deep and continue.

In the next town, Los Arcos, there was a lovely clinic open for pilgrims. I guess I must have looked pretty desperate. The first person I happened to see on a sidewalk, a young man in his 20's, took one look at me and carried me to the facility. The staff was so kind. They cleaned up my wounds, dressed and bandaged them and took an x-ray of my face. I had a small fracture of the right zygomatic bone as I had thought. Also, I suffered a mild concussion. They put some steri-strips over the avulsed skin and gave me some antibiotic ointment for it. This called for a nice hotel room, a steaming hot bathtub soak and a good night sleep. No hostels tonight. Back on the road tomorrow. I would finish the Camino with a huge black and blue eye that not even sunglasses could cover up.

8

A FOOT MASSAGE
IN AMBASMESTAS

The unexpected on the Camino is like receiving a lovely present. As you unwrap it, the joy experienced is just as good as viewing the present inside. Such was the case for me one night in Ambasmestas. After checking into my small Refugio, only 8 beds at 5 euros per night, the Hospitaller, the woman volunteering for a month at the Refugio, instructed us to go find our beds, get unpacked and organized, then return to the common area for a surprise.

As I came down the stairs, the lovely Margaret bade me to sit in a most comfortable armchair next to a table adorned with bottles of lotions and oils. She then brought out a basin of warm water and began to wash my feet. This was followed by the most wonderful foot massage I have ever received.

Here is Margaret's story. She is a practitioner of holistic medicine from Oregon. She walked the Camino three years ago and felt the calling to return to share her gift with fellow pilgrims. This is her second-year volunteering at this Refugio, and she plans to return each year for two to four weeks each time followed by walking a week or two on the Camino.

For a pilgrim, the feet get the most abuse. Bad or injured feet can put a quick halt in your trek. If you can't walk, you stop. Just like that. Margaret generously offered her talent, her skill, to help the pilgrims. That evening she individually took care of all seven of us who stayed there that evening. Bless you Margaret!

9

TAKING A DUMP
ON A HILLSIDE

While walking the Camino one often sees the warning sign of a character taking a dump and the international red circle and diagonal cross line indication that human excretion is not permitted on the trail. But...when you have to go, you have to go.

During the first few days on the Camino your body is shocked into numerous unfamiliar goings-on including sleep deprivation, physical

activity for extended periods of time, unfamiliar food and, most importantly, unfamiliar water of which you consume vast amounts. The digestive system reacts in one of two manners. Either completely shuts down or turns into Niagara Falls.

About 12 kilometers past Pamplona is the famous metal sculptures depicting pilgrims traveling either on foot or on horseback. Created by Jose' Acuña in 1996 it is perhaps the most recognizable work of art on the Caminos. If you look closely you will see the following engraved into one of the statues:

"Donde se cruza el camino del viento con el de las estrellas."

This translates as "where the path of the wind crosses that of the stars." This hilltop, as with all the hilltops in the area, have a lot of wind. Every ridge for miles in all directions are peppered with windmills as evidence.

After visiting this impressive pilgrim sculpture, perhaps the most famous pilgrims on the Camino, I began the downhill journey to Puente la Reina. The path, which is quite steep at times, makes numerous switchbacks. At several places, the path gets so steep they have built rock reinforced steps to assist the pilgrims. Because of all the rain, the slippery mud adds a substantial degree of difficulty.

Half-way down the mountain the contents of my lower intestines (you get the drift?) necessitated the immediate evacuation. The trail was moderately crowded, so I needed to find a secluded place quickly. Off to the side of this extremely steep and slippery area, hidden by a bush, take off the backpack, grab my emergency stash of toilet paper and… relief. Now then, finish up and, oops, slip, splat, tumble. I cannot believe this just happened. I find myself with my pants around my ankles after executing a backward summersault, covered in mud and my bodily fluids. The scene was so comical I burst out laughing then realized where I was. Pilgrims were descending the trail just feet away from me. I had to turn on stealth mode but could not completely stop laughing. Oh my. You know what they say, s*;t happens. Even as I write this story I am laughing!

──── ❦ 10 ❦ ────

THE MOST VALUABLE
TOOL IN MY BACKPACK

When you ask pilgrims what is their most valuable or most used item in their backpack is, there are as many items as there are pilgrims. For example, a common one is the trail map. While the Camino is well marked with yellow arrows and scallop shells, there are places where the markers are not easily seen or missing. If you take a wrong turn you could go several  kilometers in the wrong direction necessitating in backtracking. On a pilgrimage where every step is measured, backtracking is something you do not want to do.

Another valuable item is the cell phone. Not only can you keep in touch with family, you can access your GPS and track where you are and where you need to go. Also, you can book hotel rooms prior to arriving in town. Refugios and Alberges do not take reservations but you can call ahead and see if they have beds. When you get into the villages and cities you can locate businesses such as ATM's, laundry, grocery stores, and restaurants. You can also use apps that will detail historical sites and building that are a "must see" in the area.

The list goes on and on from boots, to walking sticks, to Band-Aid kits to water bottles. For me, the most important item I carried was…drum roll…my Swiss Army knife and corkscrew. I say this tongue in cheek, but I actually did use it a lot. At the end of the day, pilgrims staying in Refugios would often cook their dinner in the common kitchen. The bottle of wine they picked up to have with dinner would be great if only they could find a corkscrew. Enter the corkscrew queen stage left. Of course, after opening their bottle they were most happy to share with me.

—◦❦ **11** ❧◦—

THE WINE FOUNTAIN

The Monastery of Irache, about two kilometers from Estella and just outside of the little village Ayegui in Navarre, houses a winery that was established in 1891. Originally, the vineyards in the surrounding area were donated to the Monastery by King Sancho IV of Navarre in 1072. This Monastery was at that time also used as a hospital for pilgrims on the way to Santiago. In the 19th century the Monastery of Irache closed its doors leaving the winery and vineyards unattended.

It was only a matter of time before the value of the land and vineyards were to be recognized again and the making of Irache wine restored. Thus, in 1891 the property was purchased and the winery Bodegas Irache established. The winery owns 150 hectares of vineyards and produces both red and white wines including Tempranillo, Cabernet Sauvignon, Merlot, Chardonnay and Malvasia.

The *Codex Calixtinus*, written in the 12-century under the guidance of Pope Callixtus II, is basically a travel guide for pilgrims of the day. In the chapter containing information of the area of Navarre, the guide notes that the area is known for good bread and good wine. The monastery was evidently celebrated by pilgrims as a good place to stay the night and have a good meal with great wine.

Fast forward to 1991. The owners of the Bodegas Irache Winery, recognizing the historical significance of giving food, wine and lodging to pilgrims, opened up a section of the winery wall and put in a fountain from where the pilgrims can turn the valve and dispense wine directly from a barrel in the winery.

Most pilgrims use their scallop shell to put wine in then drink from, the scallop shell being a symbol of the Camino. Other pilgrims fill up a water bottle. Pilgrims need to take care if the day is hot and one has a thirst. The wine is good and goes down very nicely.

If one does not have a receptacle for the wine, one can just open one's mouth and turn on the spigot. Such was the case for me. I have a Camelback system in my backpack with a drinking hose, so I did not have anything to put the wine into for drinking. The winery employee who was regulating the fountain said it was OK and, in fact, encouraged me to do so.

Have you ever seen a German tour bus? If you have done any traveling in Europe, you know what I am talking about. These are luxury boats on wheels. As I'm getting my downpour of wine, a titanic sized German tour bus of senior citizens pulls up. They were amazed at seeing this sight. A wine fountain with a "real" pilgrim imbibing the red liquid. I speak German so I got a laugh at what they were saying about me. When I finally spoke to them in their language, they had a million and one questions for me. Where did I start? Is it hard? How heavy is my backpack?

If you are not a pilgrim, you are not allowed to drink from the fountain. Such was the case with these German tourists. But they could get pictures. Each couple, or group, or individual wanted a picture with the "pilgrim" drinking from the fountain. Get ready, pose, position my mouth under the spigot and, eine, zwei, drei, let the juice flow and snap the picture. After twenty or so pictures, I was feeling quite nice. Danke meine neuen Freunde -thank you my new friends!

─── 12 ───

TARTA DE SANTIAGO

I am a dessert person. I don't just like desserts, I have a passion for desserts and sweet things. My food philosophy is, *Life is uncertain, Eat dessert first.* I may joke about it but that is the genuine "me." It is not uncommon for me to go to a restaurant  and order dessert as my main course. Naturally, when I travel, I seek out all the sweet nibbles the country has to offer.

On my first Camino, when I crossed into the province of Galicia, I was introduced to a lovely torte made from ground almonds, eggs, and sugar. In the Galician language it is called Torta de Santiago and in Spanish, Tarta de Santiago. Torta, tarta, in my epicurean analysis it is simply good. Dating back to the Middle Ages, the tarta is decorated with the symbol of the *Order of the Knights of Saint James* or *Orden de Santiago*. The symbol is a cross / sword design with fleur-de-lis decoration. The combination of the cross and sword represents the military nature of the order combined with the martyrdom and decapitation of Saint James.

Ingredients

- 2 cups blanched almonds ground coarsely in a food processor
- 8 Large eggs, separated
- 1 ½ cups superfine sugar
- ¼ cup confectioners' sugar for dusting

Optional:

- Grated orange zest to taste
- Grated lemon zest to taste
- 4 to 6 drops almond extract
- Grated nutmeg to taste

Preparation

1. Beat the egg yolks with the sugar to a smooth pale cream. If using optional ingredients, add at this time.
2. Add the almonds and mix until completely incorporated.
3. With clean beaters, beat the egg whites to stiff peaks.
4. Combine the egg whites with the almond mixture. It will be thick but gently fold it in until well combined.
5. Prepare an 11-inch spring-form pan with parchment paper on the bottom. Generously coat the paper and sides of the spring-form pan with butter.
6. Pour the batter into the spring-form and place in a pre-heated oven at 350 degrees F for 40 minutes or it feels firm to the touch.
7. Let it completely cool then sprinkle with confectioners' sugar and serve.

---- ❊ **13** ❊ ----

THESE BOOTS ARE
MADE FOR WALKING

Walking is man's best medicine –Hippocrates

Perhaps the most important part of your body to take care of is your feet. After all, they are responsible for every step you take. Along the Camino, whenever you stop for a break and get a chance to visit with other pilgrims, the topic of footwear weaves its way into the conversation. Almost an obsession, the typical pilgrim can offer a myriad of discourses ranging from shoes and boots and sandals, to blisters, tendons, bruises, and bone spurs.

Many pilgrims are fervent about their choice and can pose multiple reasons why their footwear is the best and anyone using anything different is irrational. These folks obviously have, either by chance or by good fortune, found a combination that works for them. On the other hand, those who are suffering from foot problems did not listen to the experts (tongue in cheek). Wrong, wrong, and wrong. Oh, did I say wrong?

On both of my Caminos, I did not suffer any foot problems. By good fortune and some research, I found a combination that works for me. I use a hiking boot one size larger than I normally wear and I use Smartwool socks with an attached liner. I have three pair of these socks. On my walk, every time I would take a break for coffee, lunch, or snack, I would take off my boots and socks, air them out then put on a clean pair of socks. Each evening I would wash the socks and repeat the next day. This worked for me. It will not work for everyone. You just need to experiment with combinations prior to your Camino and hope you choose the best one. However, if while on the Camino you discover your combination is not working, you need to immediately go to a store in the nearest large community and purchase some different shoes or boots.

On my second Camino I went with my dear friend Lisa. For several months prior to our Camino, we trained almost daily together. We had our packs loaded the same as we would on the Camino, even carrying water. Her equipment seemed to be working well for her. However, on the third day of our Camino, Lisa began developing hot spots, primarily on her right foot. We did the padding thing, different socks, Band-Aids, but nothing helped. The next day she was in real pain and could not get her right boot on. Lisa had a pair of pink gummy shoes for wearing in the shower or around the Refugios. She put her left boot on her left foot and a pink shoe on her right. Down the trail we walked.

When you are walking daily, it is as if you are with a wave of walkers. You may not leave the same time each morning, or take the same breaks, or walk at the same speed but you often see members of "your wave." You begin to recognize these people, converse briefly with them as you pass, and even learn a few brief bits of information about them such as their name and where they are from and who they are walking with. With this familiarity comes the inherent convention of assigning monikers or nick names for them. Lisa became known as "the lady with the pink shoe." On the trail people would call out "hey pink shoe, Buen Camino."

The next day, after giving her right foot a rest, Lisa began to have trouble with her left foot. Most probably because she was walking unevenly from boot to pink shoe, she developed blisters on the left foot. Time to use the other pink shoe. At least her two shoes matched. Lisa would finish the Camino switching two or three times daily from boots to pink shoes.

---—⚜ **14** ⚜—---

FINDING THE SIGNS

When you think about it, walking across a country takes a bit of courage, some self-assurance, and a lot of chutzpah. The question most frequently asked by those not knowledgeable in the Camino is "How do you know where to go?" The answer is "You follow the Signs." That may sound simple, but it is what you do and it's not always easy.

There are basically two types of signs you must look for, the yellow arrow and the stylized scallop shell. These signs can be posted independently but are often found together. Sometimes they are easy to see, sometimes they are not. If you miss one, you can possibly walk a great distance before realizing you are no longer on the Camino.

The most iconic symbol, the scallop shell, is a visual metaphor with the lines representing the many routes pilgrims travel to Santiago. It is usually positioned with the "rays" or routes of the shell spanning out to the direction you have come from, bringing all the routes to the central point, Santiago de Compostela.

The Yellow Arrows are the creation of the parish priest of O Cebreiro, Elías Valiña Sampedro (1929-1989). Born and raised in Sarria, his passion was the history of the Camino of Santiago. Studying at the University in Salamanca, his doctoral thesis was on the Camino. In 1984 he experienced a calling, that of the importance of reviving the ancient religious trail to Santiago. Much of the original route was overgrown and impassable. However, as an articulate and educated man, he was able to convince parishes, city officials and various associations of "Friends of The Way," to begin restoring the Camino Frances.

In the late 1970's and 80's, Don Elías began marking the route using his old Citroën GS and a can of yellow spray paint. Since the color yellow was traditionally used for trail markers in many of the European countries, he probably decided the color would make the arrows more recognizable as Camino way markers. This tradition has continued to date.

Your first few days on the Camino has your head spinning in many diverse directions coping with this new activity. You are thinking about your pack, your shoes, your drinking water supply, your nourishment, where and when you are going to take a break, where you are going to stop for the night. Then, ding, ding, ding, you say to yourself, "have I seen a sign recently? Am I walking on the correct path?" After a couple of days, you get into an autopilot rhythm and the brain settles down into a mode of stillness as you walk. But, beware, don't become too complacent. Retracing one's steps is something you do not want to do. If you miss a sign that is precisely what you may be doing.

So, where do you look for these signs? I have seen then in some obvious places and some in places where you wonder what the sign person was thinking putting the sign there. Obvious places are concrete markers when the trail forks, cement sidewalks with imbedded shell and arrow markers, wooden signs painted and affixed to trees, telephone poles and buildings. Often, when you get to the larger cities, these markers do not exist. On more than one occasion I had to ask a local where the trail is.

People are generally most accommodating and happy to assist you back to the trail. On one occasion when I found myself in middle suburbia with no signs in sight, I asked a lady in a car at a stop light if she know where the trail was. She had me get in her car and drove me back the mile or so to the point where I missed the sign. That was a most welcome ride. A good rule of thumb is, when you get into a larger city, head for the main cathedral. The trail always goes by there and you will always find a sign.

I was walking through a little village a couple of days west of Burgos when I stopped at a bar for an orange juice. At one of the outdoor tables sat a group of older men in loud conversation enjoying a coffee. The bar was at a split in the road with no visible signs to direct the pilgrims. When a pilgrim or group of pilgrims went left the old men seemingly paid no attention. However, when a stray pilgrim or group went right the old men would yell. One did not have to understand Spanish to get to the gist of their yelling. They were telling the pilgrims to go left not right. If they did not turn back to make the correction one of the old men would get up and chase them down gesturing for them to come back and make the adjustment. My first thought was why the men didn't just put up a sign. Then I realized that would deprive them of this most enjoyable activity that they have probably doing every day for years.

15

KEEPING KOSHER
ON THE CAMINO

The national food of Spain is the Pig. I say that in jest, but the reality is that most everything served in restaurants, tapas bars, fast food stands and bars, has some sort of pig product in it. It has been said that you can eat every part of the pig except for the squeal and Spain is proof.

Early on in my first Camino I was in a restaurant and ordered a salad. After confirming with the waitress that it was vegetarian, I felt reasonably comfortable that I would be able to eat it. When the salad arrived, I saw that it had bacon bits on it. Calling back my waitress and in a very nice voice I told her that I thought I had received someone else's salad because I ordered a vegetarian one. She informed me that it was a vegetarian salad. There was no meat on the salad only lardons. You see, in Spain, Pig is in its own food group, not dairy, not meat, not vegetable.

So, can you keep kosher on the Camino? Yes, you can, but it takes planning, adaptability, improvisation, and a willingness to experiment. But what if you accidently or unknowingly eat something that is not kosher. To answer that question, I will turn to the Chabad Rabbis as posted on https://www.chabad.org/library/article_cdo/aid/1614932/jewish/I-Ate-Non-Kosher-Food-Now-What.htm:

While every food has its nutritional value, certain foods have the capacity to provide us with spiritual nutrition too. This is kosher eating. The Torah allows us to eat certain foods, not because they are healthy for our body, but because they are healthy for our soul.

On the other hand, non-kosher foods block the connection between body and soul, deaden our perception of holiness and desensitize us from the world of spirit.

But there is a way that non-kosher food can elevate you. This can happen when the eating of non-kosher food itself stirs you toward spiritual growth. When you regret what you have done and resolve to be extra-cautious in the future, and when you commit to being more careful in your general observance of the dietary laws, reviewing the relevant laws, then you have made the non-kosher food a means for growth.

Here is how I keep Kosher while in Spain. My primary source of food was from the small markets and grocery stores. For prepackaged foods, I looked for the Kosher symbol that I purchase at home in California. However, one does have to be careful. Just because it has the kosher certification in the US market does not mean that it will have that same certification in Spain. Before you pick up that familiar candy bar or packet of soup, look for the kosher symbol. In some of the larger markets there will be a section for "American Food" where you can get the products you are familiar with such as soda, candy, cereals and soups, all with the familiar kosher symbol.

In the smaller Refugios with a kitchen the meals are often a "team effort." As you meet your fellow pilgrims during the days of walking you begin to connect with them. Often you recognize people you saw on the trail that day, or days past, and you are all staying in the same place. It is quite enjoyable to create a meal together with each person contributing something. I usually offer to do the salad and desert since that is what I usually eat and can easily make it a kosher option. That way I know I will be able to not only contribute but have something I can eat and enjoy the companionship of my fellow travelers. Often these meals are quite good. Here are a couple of recipes for my impromptu creations.

CEVICHE SALAD

- ½ red onion sliced very thinly
- 1-pound fresh fish such as sea bass, snapper or whatever looks good at the fish monger stall. Cut into ½ inch cubes
- 1 to 2 garlic cloves finely minced
- 1 teaspoon kosher salt
- ¼ teaspoon black pepper
- ½ cup cilantro chopped
- One chili pepper seeded and chopped if desired.
- ¾ cup fresh lime juice
- 15 to 20 grape tomatoes cut in half or two medium tomatoes diced.
- One cucumber diced.
- 1 tablespoon olive oil
- One avocado diced as garnish.

After slicing the red onion, salt it generously and let stand for 15 minutes until it begins to release its liquid. This removes the bitterness resulting in a sweet textural crunch. Rinse well and squeeze dry.

Place the fish, garlic, onion, salt, pepper, chilies, and lime juice in a shallow bowl. Gently mix and put in the refrigerator for about 30 to 45 minutes. The longer you allow it to marinate the firmer and more "cooked" the fish will be.

Toss in the cilantro, cucumber and tomato and a drizzle of olive oil and lightly mix. Place slices of fresh avocado on top and serve with crackers, chips or even lettuce cups.

This next recipe is a fun one, especially for non-English speaking pilgrims, because of its funny name, Muddy Buddies. It always brought a crowd laugh as our non-American colleagues tried to say it. Regardless of the language barriers, this great desert was always a home run. The leftovers were easily packable for a snack on the trail the next day. Sometimes as I was walking I would hear "Muddy Buddies" from behind and turn to see a fellow pilgrim who had shared a communal dinner in some village where I made it.

MUDDY BUDDIES

- Nine cups of any combination of any cereal. I like a mixture of corn puffs, captain crunch, puffed rice and smashed shredded wheat. All of these come in Kosher products in most grocery stores.
- One cup crunchy peanut butter
- One cup peanuts
- One cup chocolate chips
- ½ cup butter
- 1 ½ cups powdered sugar

Melt the peanut butter, chocolate chips and butter using a microwave or stove top. Toss in all the cereal and nuts and stir to coat everything. Put the mixture in the fridge until it cools. Remove and dump into a clean sealable plastic bag. Dump in the powdered sugar, seal the bag and shake. There it is -Muddy Buddies a la Camino.

Variations on this recipe are unlimited. Try different nuts, dried fruits, even roughly crushed cookies such as vanilla wafers or shortbread. All available in stores throughout Spain.

Bon Appetite!

—❧ 16 ❧—

A SURPRISE FESTIVAL

I had heard that Logroño was a lovely place to take a rest day, just exactly what I was needing. The previous 5 or 6 days had been up and down and up and down but nothing too extreme. Beautiful walking but wearing both mentally and physically. A day of rest in Logroño sounded great. Approaching the village from the north east, the land was checkerboarded with agricultural designs which included everything edible from fruit trees to vegetables to wine grapes. What a lovely sight. Acres and acres, miles and miles, hills and valleys of edibles, or drinkables.

Coming into town, crossing over a bridge with a lovely park and river underneath, the welcome sight of an old medieval looking village was captivating. Approaching up the street from the old buildings were a group of people in medieval costume acting as if everything were normal. Conversing, wine glass in one hand and some sort of green leaf branch in the other. Did I just step through a time shift? Turn another corner and even more of the same. Everyone and everything looks as if we just landed in the 16th or 17th century.

When I get into a new town, I have learned to head for the cathedral. This is typically the central focus of a village and a great place from which to begin the search and selection of a place to stay the night. Also, it allows me the opportunity to size up the community, locate stores, restaurants, and shops that I might want to explore. This community seemed to be in some sort of festival. The streets were lined with a particular type of greenery in pots, vines, arbors, tubs, and every person had it either in their hand or stuck in their clothing or hair or hat. Naturally, I had to get one and position it appropriately in the chest

strap of my pack saying to myself that I would discover the significance at a later time. For now, I needed to find a place to stay the night.

Shrubbery in place, oriented to cathedral and old town, I commenced looking for the nights lodging. In the distance I heard a sound of…bagpipes? Wait a minute, this is Spain not Ireland or Scotland. Down the street about two blocks away was a procession coming toward me. It was a parade.

Escorted by a motorcycle police crew, the parade began with the traditional *Gigantes* and *Cabezudos*. *Gigantes* or Giants are oversize hollow figures several meters tall with a painted paper maché head and arms. The rest of the body is covered in cloth clothing. The entire structure is mounted on a person inside who manipulates the giant to swing and dance in rhythm to the band that follows. The parade usually has at least two giants, the male and female, or *giganta* and *gigantona*.

The *Cabezudos* or "Big Head" are smaller figures, no taller than the person inside, but with an oversized head. The person inside the costume uses one hand to hold the giant head and the other hand to hold a whip or pig bladder which is used to frighten children or young women.

This whole procession was followed by a Catalan shawm band. This instrument is a type of a shawm which is an oboe-like woodwind musical instrument. Hence, the sound of bagpipes. The parade lasted about five minutes, not very long. However, I was to discover these parades would happen continually throughout the day, and afternoon, and evening, and night, and late night, and late late night.

Back to the business at hand, find a bed for the night. As I turned around to begin my search, I see the familiar sign *"Albergue."* What luck! Walking into the ultra-modern hotel looking accommodations I ask if they have an available bed. Not only do they have beds available in all 8 dorm rooms at 12 euros, they have private rooms for 18 euros. Sold!!! Not that I do not want to sleep with my fellow pilgrims, snoring, farting, getting up to use the facilities all night long, but I don't. Whenever there is a private room available, I always grab it. A bed in a dorm room is typically my last option. Also, another bonus, one is allowed to book this Albergue for consecutive nights due to the festival. This is pretty much unheard of in these types of accommodations. Typically, one must check in after 2:00 or so and exit in the morning by 8:00 AM and no double dipping.

After checking into the Albergue, getting settled in and doing my obligatory laundry, I set out to find out what the festival was all about. Off to the local TI (tourist information) to get a map and printed material. This festival was called *Fiestas de San Bernabé* or Festival of Saint Barnabus, the patron Saint of Logroño. It seems that in 1521 the French had invaded Spain and were trying to conquer Logroño by laying siege to the city. The city inhabitants survived on eating fish that they caught in the river. They would sneak out under cover of night,

DR. GUYLENE GIGI TREE

past the city walls through the secret tunnels, catch the fish and return unseen. Because the area, La Rioja, was already a famous wine region, they had plenty of wine to go along with the fish. Thus, they survived until forces arrived and assisted in defeating the French. Today, the primary focus of the festival is lots of free fish and lots of free wine, everywhere. What is not to like. Never did find out about the green shrubbery.

Other information I received from the TI was a program of events including scheduled food and wine tasting, fireworks times and locations, music performances which were at numerous venues throughout the old city, and finally, a battle reenactment of the siege by the French and their defeat. What a lovely rest day.

⸺⋇ 17 ⋇⸺

LAUNDRY ON
THE CAMINO

If you take the minimalist approach to packing for the Camino as I do, clothing is one set to wear and one set to wash. Typically, my routine on the Camino is to check into my sleeping accommodation and immediately head for the shower. I hop in wearing all the clothing I am going to wash. Scrub down as I take off each item until all is clean and rinsed, including me. I then put on my second set of clothes and hang

up the wet ones to dry. If they are dry in the morning, great, they get stowed in the pack. If not, they are hung on my backpack to flap in the wind as I walk. I am not alone in doing this. One often sees fellow pilgrims in the morning walk with their underwear flapping.

My dear friend Lisa, with whom I walked the Celtic Camino, was not as diligent as I. She also had a lot more clothes than I had so didn't need to wash as often. However, when she did, it was a chore. Hence, she typically delayed the procedure until it became absolutely necessary. This necessity came about on a lovely day at a delightful Refugio in the in a little village with perhaps 4 or 5 buildings…small, very small. But a pleasant restaurant and bar and an available private room at the Refugio. The laundry facility consisted of a cement structure with a corrugated slanting surface and a cold-water spigot. Lisa needed to wash everything except her green plastic rain poncho and pink shoes as you can see in the picture.

The time of day was late afternoon. Yep, almost time for sundown and colder temperatures. While there was a drying rack outside, the clothes would never be dry by morning and, as I mentioned, green rain poncho and pink shoes. We brought all the wet clothes into our room and cranked up the heat spreading everything out wherever we could. Can you say, "yard sale?" Time for drinks in the bar then dinner then more drinks…green rain poncho and pink shoes. We were definitely the topic of conversation that evening.

18

THE CELTIC CAMINO

When you hear the words *"Camino de Santiago de Compostela"* most think of the Camino Frances. This is the most popular route but not the only one. Traditionally a Camino begins at your house wherever that might be. The Celts had a pilgrimage of sorts which took them south to the water's edge by foot, across the Atlantic by boat to the area we know today as A Coruña. From there they continued walking to their ritual site we know today as Cruz de Ferro.

The route from A Coruña to Santiago is called the Camino Ingles since it would have been the traditional route taken by pilgrims from Ireland, England, and Scotland. The route is 75 kilometers, just 25 short of the required 100 for a Compostela Certificate. Recently, the Cathedral of Santiago agreed to grant the Compostela Certificate to pilgrims who complete a minimum of 25 kilometers in Ireland then finish the remaining 75 along any of the other routes. The Camino Ingles is the most popular route in Spain for this continued journey but the routes in Ireland are many.

The route that Lisa and I took began in Dublin Ireland. What a great place to start! The St. James Gate was the western entrance to the city during the Middle Ages. During this time, the gate and the enclosed area was the traditional starting point for pilgrims from Ireland. While the gate was demolished in 1734, the walled structure and buildings remained and in 1759 was taken over by Arthur Guinness who, as we know, makes a wonderful brew. Inside the entrance of the present Guinness Brewery you can get an official sello or stamp in your pilgrim passport, thus marking the first stamp of your Camino. What a great way to begin, a beer and a stamp.

From here there are many options to walk. Christ Church Cathedral is a great choice located only 2 kilometers away. This is one of two medieval cathedrals in Dublin and well worth the walk, visit, and stamp. About 1 kilometer away is the celebrated Trinity College which contains the famous Library of Trinity College. This huge structure holds the largest collection of manuscripts and books including the famous Book of Kells. A stamp in your Pilgrim Passport is a must.

The following walks are the most popular for the beginning 25 kilometers of the Celtic Camino:

Tóchar Phádraig -35km
>   Starts in Ballintubber Abbey ends in Murrisk. This path was originally a chariot road to the seat of the Kings and Queens of Connacht. After the time of St. Patrick, pilgrims began using the road and over time it became to be called Tóchar Phádraig or St. Patrick's Causeway.

Bray Coastal Route -32km
>   Starts in Bray Sea Front and ends at St James Church, Dublin.

Boyne Valley Camino -25km
>   This is a circular route that begins and ends in Drogheda.

St Kevin's Way -30km
>   Starts in Hollywood and ends in Glendalough. As the name suggests, this route follows in the footsteps of St. Kevin through the hills of Wicklow and the monastic ruins in Glendalough. This route can be started either in Hollywood or in Valleymount.

St Finbarr's Pilgrim Path -42km

Starts in Drimoleague and ends in Gougane Barra. This two-day walk follows the footsteps of St. Finbarr who visited Drimoleague in the 6th century. You can just do the pilgrims path which begins about halfway at Gougane Barra from Carringanass Castle in Kealkill.

Kerry Camino -57km

Perhaps the most popular and one of the longer routes. Begins in Tralee and ends in Dingle.

Croagh Patrick Heritage Trail -60km

Starts in Balla ends in Murrisk. This trail is typically walked from east to west, to the Atlantic Ocean.

St Declan's Way -96km

The longest but can be done in shorter segments either direction. The two main points for starting or ending are Ardmore (Waterford) and Cashel (Tipperary).

For our Celtic Camino, Lisa and I did a combination of several trails including, Bray Coastal Route, Boyne Valley Camino, and St. Declan's Way. In total we walked well over 100 kilometers which was more than enough for our Pilgrims Credentials. We got stamps from places such as The Rock of Cashel, Abby in Innis, Dirty Nells Pub in Bunratty and several Garda stations. What a hoot. They were all so lovely to the two ladies from California walking across (I don't think they really understood what we were doing) their country asking for stamps in their wee booklets.

19

THE ROCK OF CASHEL AND TOM

My husband and I have dear friends, Mike and Irene, who were our neighbors for over 20 years in California. They were originally from Ireland and decided to move back for their twilight years. Irene was born and raised in Ennis, a small village in County Clare. Mike and Irene live about one block from the house where she was born. Within a 10-minute walk of their house one can find about 30 pubs. Needless to say, this is not only a typical Irish village, but one that should be visited.

Just a couple of blocks from the main old town area is a lovely Boutique Hotel run by Tom. During our many stays there, Tom has become a dear friend. The year that Lisa and I did our Celtic Camino, we of course stayed with Tom at the Ashford Court Boutique Hotel.* Lovely place with a great staff, immaculate rooms, and a full Irish breakfast each and every morning. Oh my.

Let me briefly characterize Tom. A giant of a man but a teddy bear. Profoundly serious but very funny. Very matter of fact but extremely accommodating. A gentle giant with a big heart and a brilliant wit. One morning over tea we were telling Tom of our plans for the day which included walking part of the loop to The Rock of Cashel. Tom said,

"Ah yes, and will ye be bringing me bach thee rock?" With a wink and a smile, we said "of course Tom." The tail of our escapade will follow a brief background of the Rock of Cashel.

Located in Cashel Town, County Tipperary, the site is a collection of medieval ecclesiastical buildings which are set on a rocky outcrop of limestone. The oldest surviving building on the Rock dates from the 12th century and includes a high cross and the ruins of a Romanesque chapel. Next to this structure is a 13th century Gothic cathedral and a 15th century castle and the Hall of the Vicars where the original Cross of St. Patrick can be found.

This whole historical collage owes its construction and survival to two of the most important persons in the history of Ireland. First was St. Patrick who arrived in Cashel in the year 432 and baptized King Aengus who became Ireland's first Christian ruler. The second person was Brian Boru who was crowned High King at Cashel in 990. He was the only king who was able to unite all of Ireland under a single ruler for any significant period of time.

So, the Rock of Cashel is not a "rock" but a rocky hill with buildings on it. But Tom said he wanted a rock and a rock we would bring him. After our walk and visit of the site, Lisa and I set off in the car on dirt roads around the area looking for the perfect rock. Narrow dirt roads, little cow or goat trails not suited for our rental car and careful scrutiny of numerous rocks and we finally we find the perfect one. Now then, how do we get this big rock in the trunk of our car. Carefully, with well-choreographed  moves, we were able to roll the monster over to the car, then, one, two, three, and up and in the trunk.

Now we had to personalize the rock. We are off to the art and craft store for paint and brushes. Supplies obtained, back to the Hotel to decorate the rock. Tom would be back at the Hotel in the early evening, so we had to hurry. With gold, silver, and copper paint the rock proclaimed, "TOM'S CASHEL ROCK." To this day it rests in front of the hotel.

*Ashford Court Boutique Hotel
Old Mill Road, Co. Clare
+353 (0) 65 689 4444
info@ashfordcourthotel.com
www.ashfordcourthotel.com

20

SANTIAGO -REALLY?

One reads numerous accounts of the emotional feelings, physical conclusion, and mental exhaustion upon reaching the destination, the Cathedral de Santiago. As the days tick off, the steps no longer counted, the focus on "making it" to the end, the mind just shuts down. No more imagining the grand entrance to the Cathedral square. No more checking the guidebook or map, just walking. No more idle mind reflections. No stop at a bar for a cup of coffee or Coca-Cola. Let's just get there. Possibly comparable to the last mile of a marathon. Tunnel vision in sepia tones.

I have made this journey two times and each time has been unique. On my first journey, I entered the city of Santiago from the east coming off the Camino Frances. I knew I would be walking in suburbia Spain, but this went on and on and on. Freeways, overpasses, roundabouts, houses, buildings, car dealerships, industrial buildings. After so many days walking in forests, green agricultural areas, flatlands and hills, this was anticlimactic. But then, just a few more kilometers and it would be OK. Can I see the Cathedral yet? No. More freeways and bypasses. One hour later, now this is looking better. The buildings are older, streets smaller. Must be getting closer.

I was so excited that I was almost there I decided not to check into my pre-booked hotel but head straight for the Cathedral. Can't be much further now. Down a cobblestone street with a central fountain, more shops, tourist area. Must be getting closer. Then, in the distance I hear a, what's that, a bagpipe? Yep. Down the steps, under an arch stands a bag-piper piping.

As I ventured down the corridor which leads to the main Cathedral square, I see a white tourist train filled to capacity with tourists all snapping pictures, and it is headed directly at me. But wait a minute, don't run me over. I am a Pilgrim. The square was filled with the tourist mobs being led by the director holding the umbrella or flag or sign. I wanted to scream BUT THIS IS MY CAMINO!!! Go away. I want to experience the moment. Bubble burst, I turn around and go find my hotel.

Since then I have spoken to many fellow pilgrims who have had similar feelings upon arriving at the Cathedral. You have such big expectations and when they fall short, way short, there is a bit of a disenchantment for the experience. My second time, probably because I knew what to expect, was much more enjoyable. Bottom line, go with no perceived expectations and you will not be disappointed. I'm not sure if that's possible but it sounds good.

After I checked into my hotel and got my bearings, a good night's sleep and hearty breakfast, I set off to check out all the other routes that come into the city. The route I had taken, the Camino Frances, was miles and miles of suburbia. I wanted to know if the other entrances to the city would be any different.

My first venture were the routes that approach from the North. These routes would be the Camino Inglés (the English Way) and the Camino Primitivo (the Original Way). The Primitivo which begins in Oviedo on the north Atlantic coast, joins up with the Camino Frances in Melide. This means the last 52.7 kilometers are the same as the Camino Frances hence walking the same route into Santiago. No need to walk that one. Been there…done that.

The Camino Inglés begins either in Ferrol or A Coruña. Both routes join up at Bruma, about 40 kilometers north of Santiago. I walked about 20 kilometers of this route in reverse heading north out of Santiago. After leaving the old city, the first 5 kilometers or so was industrial, similar to that of the Camino Frances. However, the landscape turned into a beautiful green expanse with lovely farmhouses and structures. On this short trek in reverse I saw perhaps a couple dozen pilgrims. Most were rather puzzled as to why I was going the wrong way. If they asked, a brief explanation confirmed I was in a different mind-set than they.

My next place to explore were the routes that enter Santiago from the south, that of the Via de la Plata and the two routes coming up from Portugal. Again, starting my backward walk from the Cathedral in Santiago, the routes all converge just south of the train station. From the old city, just a short walk through the commercial section then across the overpass of the train tracks and you are pretty much out of the city. Much better approach to Santiago.

In brief, here are my thoughts. If you are coming in from the Camino Frances, expect many kilometers of not very pleasant walking on concrete with lots of traffic. If you have the time, circle around northwest and approach the city from the north. Much nicer walking conditions and you will enjoy the last kilometers of your Camino as you finish. The best route, in my opinion is coming in from the south. Green rolling hills, farmland, nice walking path, minimal urban sprawl and downtown commercial city for only for the last couple of kilometers.

—✦ **21** ✦—

ALONE

We're born alone, we live alone, we die alone. Only through our love and friendship can we create the illusion for the moment that we're not alone. -Orson Welles

I often get asked if I was afraid going alone or why I went alone, and, the one year I took a friend, did I enjoy that more? The answer is quite complex but as valid as the question is. You see, no matter how many people are in your group, the journey ultimately is done alone. If you are unable to do it alone, you will not be able to do it with a group. I believe that you must first be comfortable by yourself before you can be comfortable with a friend.

Let me begin an explanation with the day to day activities and why it is nice to go alone. In the morning when you awake, you have a different situation, unfamiliar surroundings, unfamiliar location. You may be dressing and packing in the dark. You may have a kitchen facility to grab a quick bite of something and cup of coffee, but you may not. You may not have had a good night's sleep due to snoring or other disturbances during the night. You may awake fully rested and just want to get back out on the trail. If you are with a partner or several, the group must converse, discuss the options and come up with a consensus before acting. If you are alone, you just do what you need to do and move on to the next task.

In my Camino adventures I saw many good friends, many couples and many families completely blow up over seemingly insignificant issues. Travel is stressful. Let me say that again. Travel is stressful. This is not a 5-star resort carefree vacation. There are is no plans, no time commitment, no itinerary, no guarantee of food or water or bed when you want it. Many personalities just cannot cope in that type of situation. My husband is one of those travelers. He loves to travel, but not this type. He says, "honey, you go and have a good time" and I do.

The people I have seen on the Camino who have had a bad experience, and there are many, are discovering that they just can't cope in this type of unstructured situational travel. I chanced to meet a family, husband, wife and two teenage siblings one boy and one girl. They came in late to the Auberge after what must have been an incredibly stressful day. After going to their assigned beds and getting their belongings organized, amidst much grumbling, the girl went to the common room and put in her earbuds. The boy went out back and sulked in a lawn chair throwing pebbles. Mom gathered up all the laundry and began organizing the washing. Dad pulled out his tablet and began planning the route for the next day. Oh, my goodness. Are we having fun yet?

The reality is that if you travel with another person you must acknowledge that you could be with that person 24/7. Even if this is your spouse of 40 years, the intense time alone is unremitting. When my friend Lisa and I decided to do the Celtic Camino together I explained this to her. We talked about it and agreed that we would both be comfortable with separating at any time either of us needed to with no questions asked. She could not have been a better travel partner. On the trail, if she wanted to walk more slowly than I did, it was OK. We met up in the next village or rest stop. If I wanted to go walk around the town in the evening and she didn't, that was OK. Just because you are on the Camino with another person does not mean you are tied to them by your wrists.

Lisa and I were taking a coffee break one mid-morning and sat down at a table next to a young lady with an ace bandage on her foot and a pair of crutches next to her backpack. Of course, we immediately started up a conversation with her. Newlyweds, from one of the southern states, the couple were on a trip the two of them had planned for a long time. They were both recently graduated from college with job potentials in the fall so their summer was free. Sounded like the perfect free-spirited honeymoon. Except, on day two of their Camino she stumbled and sprained her ankle. It was so bad she could not walk on it. X-rays at the local clinic evidenced no breaks or fractures, just a very bad sprain.

When issues such as this confront a relationship, the true colors come out. This outcome was profoundly positive. She and her husband together decided that he would continue walking and she would take public transport. They kept in touch by cell phone. She would meet him at his lunch stop. Then she would arrive at their end of the day destination and secure lodging. With a glass of wine in hand and some tapas, she was there to greet him as he arrived in town. We saw this couple on many occasions over the next week or so. Just gives you that warm heart lovely feeling!

Later in the same Camino we met a delightful sister – brother team. He walked fast and she walked slow. They also mutually agreed to walk their own Camino at their own pace. He would walk a couple of days at his pace then, either take transportation back to where she was or take a rest day to wait for her. In so doing they both walked the Camino together but at their own pace. On the last day of the Camino, he waited a day for her to catch up so they could do the entrance to Santiago together.

—❈ 22 ❈—

ENTREPRENEURS

In some areas of the Caminos, villages or towns are quite far apart. If you run out of water, bummer. If you are hungry and do not have a snack, double bummer. The locals are aware of the places where one needs fortification, and the next town is quite far away. They have equipped their van, car or truck and set up shop in the middle of nowhere. Some of these vendors offer the bare minimum while others are overstocked with everything one could need. Some charge higher than normal prices while others offer their food and drink "donativo" or pay what you can by donation.

Out in an agricultural area, I came upon a farmer with cherry trees. He and his crew were harvesting the luscious fruit which to me looked like heaven in a red package. Just as I was to the end of the orchard, I saw a little stand. This kind farmer had set out baskets of cherries with a sign that read "*Toma lo que necesites. Buen Camino Pellegrino*" take what you need. Good Camino Pilgrim. How lovely and how delicious!

23

MUSIC IN PAMPALONA

It had been another long day. Arriving in Pamplona was an adventure I was looking forward to but, oh I was tired. As I was walking down the main street in the old town, I heard a live piano playing. It was in the lobby of a grand hotel. I had been staying in hostels and B and B's up to this point and this 5-star hotel was something I was not planning to stay in. But, what would it hurt to just go in and check out the afternoon performance?

Grubby and with backpack and muddy boots I stepped into the luxurious lobby. My husband often teases me about my lack of inhibition. However, my willingness to venture into the forbidden was a blessing. I went to the anti-room off the lobby where the piano was. Took off my backpack and found a comfortable chair. When the waiter came up to take my drink order, without a second thought, I ordered a white wine. This came with a lovely assortment of tapas including toasts with tomatoes, grilled eggplant with fancy toothpicks and a mixture of various local olives. Yum. Another glass please. This came with more tapas.

After this wonderful dinner of tapas, wine and live music, I needed a bed. I went up to the front desk and asked if they had an available room for the night. The receptionist said that they had a cancelation for a suite and, since I was a Pilgrim, I could have the room for the price of a single. Really? Wow!!!

Stepping into the elevator with the bellboy carrying my backpack, we arrived at the designated floor and room. As he opened the door my breath was taken away. A lovely suite with a picture window overlooking the old city, I had a living room, kitchen and bedroom with white linen and plump pillows. Thanking the bellboy and handing him some euros, I ventured into the bathroom. A bathtub like a swimming pool with bubbling jets and lots of bubble bath, I knew where I was headed soon along with my laundry.

Many have often repeated the phrase "The Camino Provides." Yes, it does. This was exactly what I needed. If I had not heard the piano playing. If I had not walked into the Hotel. If I had not followed my curiosity, then I would not have had a singularly wonderful and memorable night on the Camino. By the way, the wine and room cost me about $40.

—✠ 24 ✠—

ATM's

While Spain is a first world country, the countryside with its numerous villages and small towns seem like a world of the past. Realizing that many of the villages you pass through on a Camino route have a population of less than 50, ATM's are scarce. Most establishment along the Camino only deal in Euro. No credit cards. Therefore, your bank card and an ATM machine must be used every time you are in a big city.

Here is a brief detailing of a typical day on the Camino and where one needs to have money. Getting up early in the morning, pack the bag and take off. No money needed but hopefully you have a banana or apple from yesterday that you can eat as you walk and watch the sunrise. Mid-morning, 9 or so, time to find a bar and get a bite to eat. Coffee, orange juice and a pastry will cost about 4 euro. Mid-day and it is time for lunch. Go to a market somewhere and get some cheese, bread, fruit, chocolate bar, can of coke or juice, perhaps

6 euros. Early afternoon and time for another rest at a bar. Perhaps a coke and a slice of cake, 4 euros. Time to stop for the day and check into the Refugio for the night. A bed in the dorm is 10 euro and the evening meal 12 euro. That totals about 36 euro. Round that up to 40 euro to be safe. Now let's say you are in a large city with an ATM, but the next city is a 4 day walk ahead. Easy-peasy. You need to draw out 160 euro. I would always round up so I would get an even 200 euro. Believe me, you do not want to run out of cash. On the other hand, you do not want to travel with more cash than you will need for safety reasons.

There are a few basic rules in Europe for using US debit and credit cards. The worst mistake that first timers make is the PIN code. In the US, the banks allow you to use up to 5 letters or numbers. In Europe, you may only use 4 and the keypads only display numbers. This little detail of setting up your PIN code before you leave can save you a bundle of distress.

One afternoon as I was walking into a moderate sized village in the Galicia region, I noticed a commotion involving a group of young persons, obvious pilgrims, gathered around an ATM machine outside of a bank. They were speaking American English, so I stopped to see what was going on. It seemed the young lady had stopped to withdraw some cash using her debit card and, not knowing she needed a 4-digit PIN had tried to use her 5-digit PIN. After 3 unsuccessful attempts, the machine froze retaining her card. This was a Sunday afternoon. I assume she ended up waiting until the bank opened on Monday to rectify the situation. There were 5 in the group and this was their second day on the Camino. I hope they enjoyed the extra day!

Most banks charge a flat fee for a cash withdrawal. Let's say the fee is $4. If you take out 20 euro, your US bank charges you 4 dollars. If you take out 200 euro, your US bank still only charges you 4 dollars. So, it makes sense to take out the maximum amount you think you will need.

When you do need to use an ATM machine go to one at a bank. You typically will only have to pay the fees from your US bank. Do not use the ATM's at the train station or shopping mall. These private machines charge you an additional service fee that is often ludicrous. Also, only use your debit card not your charge card. The charge card will have additional fees which you will only discover when you look at your card statement upon returning home.

25

SHARING THE ROAD

When you leave the larger cities, and there are only a couple of them, the trails are rural. Very rural. One never knows who or what you will be sharing the road with. Milk cows, or rather the dairy industry, is very large in Spain especially in the Galicia region.

The cows get milked in the morning, then turned out in pastures during the day then back for milking and supplemental sustenance. The routes for turning them out in the morning and bringing them back in the evening are the same roads that cars use, tractors use, motorcycles use, and yes, pilgrims use. It is not uncommon to have a group of cows walk past you on the road at least once a day in some village.

Cows are motivation driven animals. They know in the morning they are going out for a day of munching on that yummy grass. They are free to wander slowly eating anything they want. On the return journey, they are motivated to get that milk out of their udders. It has been building up all day and starting to become uncomfortable. Also, after the relief of milking, they get a snack. What a life! The point is you do not have to worry about the cows strolling down the roads. They have no desire to investigate you. They are on a mission and nothing will distract them.

Now then, let's talk about the geese. Geese attacks are not a myth. These are the meanest waterfowl species alive. They are not just mean and nasty; they can seriously injure people or other animals. They are also very messy and gross, exceedingly loud and well, just plain rude. If you ever see a few  of these guys strolling down the road, hide, but do it slowly. Sudden or unexpected running will trigger them in your direction.

So why are they so mean? This behavior is because, as a bird, they are very large and extremely clumsy. They cannot hide easily when threatened so they resort to aggression as their primary form of defense. If you do get one of these birds coming at you and you cannot get away, become bigger and badder than they are. Stamp your feet. Clap your hands. Make a bigger noise than they do. You will look pretty silly but, hey, it is better than getting maimed by a couple of geese.

Another form of creature you will meet on the rural roads will be THE BIG GREEN MONSTERS. These are the agricultural farm machinery. They are loud, move slowly, but take up all the road. When you realize that one is coming, your best bet is to find some place to get completely off the road and just wait. They go awfully slow, and the operators are most courteous. Just realize that it's their road, not yours.

I must comment on one more thing we share the road with. That is the pilgrims on bicycles. Shall I repeat that? The pilgrims on bicycles. I think before they allow a pilgrim to use a bike for their Camino, they need to insist they do a day or two on foot. Then they will understand just how terrifying this pilgrim bicycle team can be.

Imagine this. It is a peaceful morning. You are walking in a beautiful wooded area on a narrow path. You have been all alone for the better part of an hour or so. Then, suddenly, with no warning, a group of spinning wheels, bright color shirts and embarrassingly stretched pants, come whizzing by at 15 or 20 mph. You barely have time to step off the one-meter wide trail as they speed past. They just don't get it. Oh well. Buen Camino.

26

GLASSES? CONTACT LENSES? BOTH?

According to the Vision Council of America, approximately 75% of adults wear some sort of vision correction. Of these, 64% wear eyeglasses and 11% wear contact lenses. The contact lens users typically also wear glasses but that is not accounted for in the numbers. I am one of the 75 percenters. I wear glasses in the morning until I get my contacts in, then put the glasses back on in the evening. So where am I going with all of this? All that vision paraphernalia is heavy. Cleaning solutions, glass cases, glasses, eye drops, storage cases. When every fraction of an ounce in your backpack is accounted for, is there any way to lighten weight of the vision stuff?

Obviously, being able to see is important. Here is how I cut down on the weight while using both contacts and glasses. The contact lenses I use are the daily ones. If I use one pair per day, on a six-week trip that is 84 little packets of lenses. You do not need saline solution since the lenses are packed in enough liquid to swish them around and pop them in. I put half of the supply in a prepackaged small box addressed to myself C/O a town at the halfway point on my Camino. When I landed at the airport in Spain and retrieved my backpack, I got out the package and posted it. Three weeks later, I went to the designated post office and got my supply of fresh contact lenses. My regular glasses are transitional lenses so when I was wearing them, I did not need sunglasses. However, when I had my contacts in, I needed nonprescription sunglasses. So, I took two pair of glasses.

I am an early riser and would often get up and out before the sun. I typically did not take the time to put in the contact lenses first thing in the morning. I used my regular glasses with the transitional lenses which worked great in the early sunrise hours. Then, at mid-morning coffee break I would go to the ladies' room and put in my contact lenses along with doing my morning wash-up. Love those bars and am always most appreciated facilities.

27

CHARGING THE PHONE

Mobile phones are the best. Whatever did we do before them? This one item replaces maps, books, coins, or tokens for telephones (yes, I remember those days). The little 4-ounce device replaces perhaps ½ to 1 pounds of weight. But what happens when you run out of juice or there is no cell service?

At home, I charge my phone at night. It functions great all day long. However, on the Camino I use it a lot. I have a GPS app that shows where I am walking. An app to find lodging for the night. An app for language translation. An app for learning of the history of buildings, churches, cathedrals, and other interesting sights along the way. An app for discovery of what things I should see in each village as well as along the way. An app for the history of the area. I take pictures and videos. I call my husband back in California. I post to Facebook. My phone gets a lot of use.

I learned a hard lesson early on in my first Camino. It was a travel day, getting from Biarritz to Saint Jean Pied du Port. In the best of days, this journey is very tricky. You land in the airport. No big deal except the airport was being remodeled. The bus stop to get the shuttle to the train station in Bayonne is nonexistent. Public transport is the only option and it is raining. The phone is being used for everything from maps, to locations of bus stops, bus stop timetables and routes, to translation. The phone is almost dead and there is no place to plug in. The choices are to find a café for coffee and plug in for a while or try to figure this out the old fashion way. I opted for the latter and made it to the proper train station where I immediately plugged in.

Because of this learning experience every time I stop, even for 5 minutes, if there is a plug, I plug in. I never had that problem again. As far as cell coverage, I never was in a position where I did not have excellent coverage. When I stopped at a café or restaurant, I would first ask for their Wi Fi code. By the way, in Spain it is pronounced "wee fee." If you say Wi Fi, they have no idea what you are talking about. Once I logged into their Wi Fi, I was able to access everything, e-mail, post to Facebook, download information I would need later in the day or the next day. Yep, phones are great!

—※ 28 ※—

WHY DO I ALWAYS SEEM TO HAVE A GLASS OF SOMETHING IN MY HAND?

After returning from my Caminos, the fun task of sorting through all my photos consumes weeks. I did several postings daily on Facebook but a lot of photos on my phone are personal. As I sort through them, it seems that every photo of me I am either holding a glass of wine, coffee, orange juice and always have something yummy to eat in front of me. That is because...I did a lot of that. Eating, drinking, traveling. They all roll together into a lovely bottle of *chateau du bliss*. Seriously, the wine and food of Spain is outstanding.

First of all, let's talk about the wine. I am from Northern California. My husband and I are wine fanatics. A perfect day of leisure for us is traveling an hour West and stopping in at several wineries in Napa or Sonoma. We are dedicated wine enthusiasts. Each wine tells its own story. The earth, the grower, the vintner, the enologist. Some wines are more to our liking than others, but we appreciate them all.

In Spain, I did not have a single glass of wine that was not amazing. The house wines in the restaurants and bars were very nice. The premium labels, oh my, delightful. The most amazing thing was they were so reasonably priced. Most glasses of wine were 2 or 3 euros. Added to this a pinchos or two and it made for a lovey dinner.

In most villages along the Caminos, the restaurants serve what is called a "Pilgrim Meal." This is a three-course meal, typically served family style and usually costing less than 10 euros. It consists of a starter such as soup or salad with bread, main course which is a protein, starch, and vegetable, then desert, a flan or pastry. Also, unlimited wine! It is usually served in a carafe, so you have no idea of the label or even the specific varietal, but it was always great. Typically, the red was a Tempranillo while the whites were Albariño. As with all wines, you can taste the basic varietal but the nuances from the enologist was always a delight to enjoy.

29

THE BEST ORANGE JUICE ANYWHERE

It was my second day on the Camino and, mid-morning, as I walked into a village, I noticed a woman in a bar (café) cutting oranges in half then manually turning them on a juicer extracting a beautiful golden orange juice. I had to stop and get some. Heading into the open-air seating area, taking off my pack and locating an appropriate place to place it along with my poles, I ventured over to the bar to place my order. In my best Spanish I asked for a small glass of orange juice. She kind of chuckled at me and said she only had one size. I told her that was fine and thank you very much. She proceeded to select 6 lovely oranges, cut them in half and begin the ritual of extracting the juice. After a couple of minutes, she presented it to me and asked for 2 euro.

Taking my large glass of cold, freshly squeezed orange juice over to a table, I sipped a bit of heaven in a juice glass. Oh my, how do I describe this. It had large chunks of pulp but none of the bitter membrane. The juice was sweet with a perfect bite of orange tartness. This was the best orange juice I had ever had! I knew it must have been a singular chance, so I enjoyed the moment.

In the Refugio that evening, while visiting with other pilgrims, I shared my experience of the outstanding orange juice. They all had similar stories but at different bars. What, really, does this lady franchise? I was just learning of the famed orange juice of Spain. You can get it in most bars. You just have to look for a large bucket or basket of oranges and a hand juicer. If you don't speak Spanish, just point. The juicer person will understand.

Orange juice became a daily ritual for me around 9 or 10 every morning. One morning I was in El Ganzo and, of course, had to stop in at the Cowboy Bar. I did not see any implements for making fresh orange juice, so I asked if they had any. My Spanish is good enough to realize that the proprietor was making fun of me and telling me that his juice in a can was just as good if not better. I quickly made my exit and walked on to the next village. Rabanal Del Camino not only had fresh squeezed orange juice, but very nice people working the apparatus.

— 30 —

FIRST CLASS OR...?

When I was young and wild, traveling on a shoestring was OK. I remember my first trip to Europe, packed like sardines in the back of the aircraft. It was the most I could afford. That was then, this is now. I can afford first class and do just that, fly only first class when taking an international flight.

It is so nice to get to sleep in a flat bed with sheets and a duvet. It's nice to order your meal from a menu and have real china and proper cutlery. It's nice to be able to get up, walk around, get an espresso or glass of champagne anytime you feel like it. Then, when you arrive at your destination, you have had a good night's sleep, and are ready to begin the adventure. On the return trip, you are tired after the long trek. Days and weeks of traveling takes a lot out of you. It is so nice to be able to stretch out on that full-length flat bed and sleep.

Typically, walking the Camino is the extreme opposite of flying first class. You are wearing the same clothes every day. You don't know when and where you will sleep. You don't know when or if you will eat properly. You live moment to moment with no expectations. I find this type of travel very nice, actually quite enjoyable. But I want my first-class seat to get there and return.

I have had fellow pilgrims criticize me for "not being completely of the pilgrim spirit." Wait a minute, just because I fly first class means I'm not a real pilgrim? Hum…that does not make sense. We are all pilgrims if we are on a Camino. It does not matter where we start, how we go, what type of lodging we use or how much we carry. If we are walking, we are a pilgrim on a Camino.

I met a group of young women carrying small daypacks, dressed impeccably, make-up perfect, hair in place. They were using a backpack transport service to schlepp their luggage from town to town, hotel to hotel. They were having fun. Not burdened with a heavy backpack, not stressing about where they would stop for the night and have dinner. Enjoying a hot shower or bath, a nice hotel bed with a lovely breakfast in the morning. Nothing wrong with that. They have figured out what their needs are and how to fulfill their requirements for the trip. Their Camino is just as valid as anyone else's.

I also encountered two lovely couples in their mid-twenties who had figured out what their needs were. The husbands were in good athletic shape and were enjoying the physical challenges of walking at a good clip. It was almost a competitive challenge for them, but they enjoyed it. On the other hand, the wives had figured out what they needed. They walked a much slower pace. When they got to a village, they enjoyed looking at the shops, stopping in at cathedrals, sitting at a café and having a coffee and generally playing the tourist. When the husbands finished walking for the day they would call or text the wives who would hop in a taxi and meet up with the spouses. Again, they are all pilgrims and have been courageous enough to do what they needed to do.

The most unusual pilgrim I saw was a dog with her human. A most adorable little female border collie mix with a big loving personality. The little dog had a Pilgrim Passport and was getting it stamped each time her human did. The little dog was doing a rather good job of keeping up. When the human companion saw that the dog was fatiguing, she would carry the little one in a baby sling worn on her front. I saw the two several times on the Camino but not in Santiago. I wonder if the little dog got a Compostela?

---- ❧ **31** ❧ ----

WATER FOUNTAINS
FOR PILGRIMS

On both of my Caminos, I have not had a problem in finding and having enough water at all times. Since these are the ancient Camino routes, the primitive settlements always provided water for village inhabitants as well as pilgrims with water fountains. These are not only in the main town square but at intervals along the Caminos. There usually is a sign or plaque telling of the origin of the fountain or group or persons who continued to maintain it. There will also be a sign letting you know that the water is OK to drink. This sign will read *"agua potable."* If it says *"agua non potable"* or *"agua sin garantia sanitaria"* do not drink it.

If for some reason you don't want to drink the water from the fountains you can purchase water. Every store along the way sells bottled water. If you run out along the trail, just stop off at a market or small store and buy some. If this purchased water bottle runs out, just find the next water fountain and fill it up. Also, when you stop at a bar for coffee or coke, ask the counter person to fill your water bottle. They are always most happy to help.

I prefer to use a camelback. For those of you unfamiliar with the device, it is a water bladder that fits in the back panel of the backpack with a tube and a valve at the end which drapes over your shoulder and clips onto the front shoulder strap. When you want to drink, just put the tube in your mouth, bite down and sip. You don't need to stop and get out a water bottle, just sip as you walk. Whenever I stop at a café or bar, I typically will take out the bladder and have the person working the counter fill it up with ice. As the ice melts along the way I always have cold water. It has worked well for me, but some prefer the water bottle.

32

MUSICOLOGICAL
DISCOURSE

In my professional life, I am a musician. Actually, both my husband and I are musicians. We both play French Horn. For the last 40+ years we have played for various orchestras locally in Northern California as well as in Europe, primarily France and Italy. I have a Ph.D. in Music, so I am also involved in music education. Over the years I have published many scholarly articles for musicological publications, interesting to me and not many others. Don't worry, I do not plan to bore you my dear reader with a tome on trivial minutiae. Rather, I hope to provide you with some background information of the wonderful Galician musical tradition with the intent to help you better appreciate the sounds, instruments, people, and performance.

When most people think of the music of Spain, what typically comes to mind is Flamenco guitars and dancing. That is true in the south, but up in the north regions of the peninsula, the music is nothing like that at all. If you look at a map, you can see the close proximity of northern Spain to Ireland. The ancient Celts spread out from Scotland and Ireland to inhabit the area ca. 900 BCE. Their historical evidence lasted throughout the Roman and even into Germanic expansions in that area.

With this connection to the Celtic people, it is only natural that the instrument and music tradition of Ireland and Scotland would influence the developing music of Galicia. A prime example of this is the Galician bagpipe which is called a *gaita*. This word is also used in the Spanish language to describe something that is disagreeable or annoying. How apropos. When compared to the Scottish or even the Irish bagpipes, the gaita is higher pitched and typically plays more upbeat rhythms and melodies.

Now, we are going to get into some technical stuff but, bear with me, it is interesting. The conventional keys of the gaita are D, C, and Bb. The instruments can have 1, 2 or 3 drone pipes. Those are the ones that stick up and over the left shoulder of the player. As in all mouth-blown bagpipes, the player inflates the bag using a tube with a one-way valve that allows the air to go in but not out. This reservoir of air is forced through the chanter with steady pressure from the left arm. The chanter, that part of the instrument that the player covers and uncovers the fingerholes, is fitted with a double reed. There are seven finger holes placed on the front of the chanter, three for the left hand, four for the right, and one at the back for the left thumb. By using techniques like cross-fingering and half-holing, a complete chromatic scale can be played. As with any musical instrument, the longer the tube, the lower the pitch of the note. The shorter the tube, the higher the pitch. As the player covers the holes on the chanter, making the tube longer, the pitch becomes lower.

This bagpipe instrument may be played solo, in duet or trio, or in vary large groups. Large group performances often include percussion instruments including a *tamboril* which is a snare-drum-like instrument, and a bass drum. Other instruments that are often used in traditional Galicia music include the hurdy-gurdy, tambourine, pandeiro (a type of square drum with jingles on the inside), the accordion and various idiophones (percussion instruments where the sound is made by rubbing or hitting).

The music of Galicia encompasses recognizable melodic types and rhythms but puts a distinctive sound or character, creating a unique style of music. *Muiñieras* are jigs in 6/8 time that are very jaunty and energetic. The *Alalas* are tunes that are short, slow, and often have vocal accompaniment. *Alboradas* are morning love songs, usually a poem about lovers separating at dawn. *Fandangos* are slower tunes, typically in 3/4 or waltz time, and are often danced to. The *Carballesas* closely resembles a hornpipe, fast, agile, and jovial.

Now then my dear reader, when you are in Galicia and you hear folk music you will feel overjoyed that you know what the instruments are and the music they are playing. Well, if not, go have some more wine and pinchos. It's all good.

— ❧ **33** ❧ —

OLIVES

With the pig being the number one food in Spain, olives definitely rank number two. I like olives, but, well what can you do with them other than spear them on a toothpick and swizzle them in your martini, or put the black ones on your fingertips. My adventures in Spain expanded my knowledge and appreciation of the fruit in ways previously thought unimaginable.

This little fruit first became cultivated between 6,000 to 8,000 years ago in Asia Minor. From there it spread to the places around the Mediterranean basin including Iran, Syria, and Palestine. About 3,000 years ago the emerald berry producing tree found its way to the northern parts of the Mediterranean including Greece, Italy, France, and Spain. As they say, the rest is history.

In Spain there are over 260 different varieties of olives. They are classified by varietal as well as defined by how ripe they are when harvested. This ripeness is seen in their coloring. The greener the olive fruit, the less ripe it is. As the fruit ripens it turns dark purple or black. It is the only food that combines the five basic tastes, sweet, salty, bitter, sour and umami. They are also the only fruit that cannot be eater directly off the tree. If you have ever tried this, you will not ever do it again.

While there are numerous varieties of olives, one will find four types commonly used as table olives. Try these first and you are sure to get hooked. It will lead you into the chasm of the gourmet grocery back home on a culinary quest for a mouthful of ecstasy.

Manzanilla -these are a medium-size olive with an even flesh-to-pit ratio. If you ask for Spanish olives at the grocery store back home, this is what you will probably get. This greenish brown olive is brine-cured and has a firm texture. The flesh has a slight almond flavor with a bit of a bitter or smoky note. The manzanilla olive is generally pitted and stuffed with garlic or pimento. These are the ones typically used in martinis.

Gordal -These olives are exceptionally large with a small pit that is easily removed. They are picked green and brined. The name *Gordal* means "the fat one." These are primarily produced in the province of Seville, so they are often referred to as *Gordal Sevillana*. It has a low oil content so is not used for olive oil, only as a table olive. The size makes them great for stuffing. Just slice in half, take out the pit and stuff with contrasting ingredients including cheese, orange or other citrus fruit, nuts, or peppers. They are also great when stuffed with cheese, rolled in breadcrumbs, and fried. A very versatile olive which goes with just about everything.

Hojiblanca -This thick skin olive has a very firm flesh and is one of the more popular black table olives. The name hojiblanca means "white leaf" referring to the underside of the leaf which is white. Because the flesh is so firm it is often used in cooking. They are frequently used in stews or marinades. They are picked late so the color is light purple to black. The olive has an aroma reminiscent of grass, pleasant taste of almond-like notes with a moderate hint of bitterness.

Cacereña -this olive is much milder than most of the typical Spanish olives making them a perfect introductory olive to the novice such as myself. The Cacereña olive is picked at an advanced stage of ripeness. By leaving them on the tree until they are completely black, the olives oxidize which causes them to lose their bitter and vegetal flavors. They are so ripe when picked that the harvester just runs the upturned hand down the branch to dislodge the fruit.

The best way to enjoy olives, according to the locals, is to enjoy them alone with a wine or beer. When you go to a bar and order a drink, you will almost always get olives in some fashion. Often just a dish of olives but sometimes served as a tapas or small bite.

In a small bar in Portomarin, I had the best olive tapenade I had ever had. It went very well with the Young Tempranillo. This is a Tempranillo wine that typically receives less than one year of aging. They are spicy, hearty and tart. An excellent companion with the tapenade. I was so overwhelmed with the combination that I made inquiry about the tapenade recipe. I was informed that the mother was back in the kitchen making it every day as did her mother and her mother, etc. I asked if I could learn of the recipe. The dear woman was so gracious and invited me into the kitchen to show me how to make it. Her secret to this outstanding tapenade was not using the traditional ingredient, anchovies. This seems to allow the true olive taste to take place center stage with no fishy taste. After playing around with ingredients we have in California, this is what I have come up with. Always a crowd pleaser but not as good as the one I had that night in Spain.

Ingredients

- 3 cloves of garlic, peeled
- 1 cup olives (I like to use the Cacereña)
- 2 tablespoons capers
- 3 tablespoons chopped fresh parsley
- 2 tablespoons lemon juice
- 2 tablespoons olive oil
- Salt and fresh ground pepper to taste

Place the garlic cloves into the food processor and pulse to mince. Add the olives, capers, parsley, lemon juice and olive oil and blend until you achieve the desired texture. Season to taste and put it in a serving bowl. Serve with crusty bread, crackers, or pita triangles.

— 34 —

TO POLE OR NOT
TO POLE

I do not know why, but often the topic of walking poles is a dinner conversation on the Camino. There are three types of pole / pole less walkers. Those who don't use poles. Those who use one pole. Those who use two poles. They all seem to have their valid arguments as to why their method is the best. So, how does one decide what to do before commencing a Camino?

Let's start off with why poles are used. The primary purpose of trekking poles is to enhance stability and provide support on all types of terrain. They can assist you in crossing over difficult terrain such as rocks, water, steppingstones, and slippery ground surface. If used properly, they take strain and pressure off the ankles, knees, and hip joints. If you are using double poles, you would use them in an oppositional movement to your step. If using one pole, decide which hand you want to use and place the pole in step with the opposite foot. If using one pole, the pole can be changed to the other hand as desired. This single walking staff is most effective when used on relatively flat terrain and with little or no load on your back.

Here is why I like to use two poles. First of all, I love to look around at everything as I walk. This means I often do not see where I'm walking or what obstacle is coming up in my path. My double walking poles have saved me numerous times from potentially disastrous situations. The walking paths on the Caminos are not flat and straight. You have windy paths, grassy trails, rocky up and downs, small streams to cross, large rocks to navigate. The poles are just an extra measure of security to keep your balance. I like them and use them.

Choosing the correct trekking poles is an art unto itself. Here are the basics. You want the poles to be at a height that will put your elbows at a 90-degree angle when you hold the poles with the tips on the ground near your feet. Often, trekking poles come in adjustable lengths that enable you to adjust the height to best suit your terrain. I find the adjustable pole to be most accommodating to my needs. If you are on a long uphill section, you can shorten the poles to a comfortable height relative to the slope. For a long downhill section, lengthen the pole by about 5 to 10 cm. In so doing your body will be kept more up upright for better balance. If you are traversing a sloped hillside, you can shorten the uphill pole and lengthen the downhill pole.

When you go shopping for poles plan to be overwhelmed by all the varieties and gadgets they offer. If you have unstable hips or knees a nice feature is shock absorbing poles. These have an internal spring mechanism that can be turned on or off as needed. Ultralight poles are best for the Camino walk where weight matters a great deal. A pair of poles that weigh in under 1 pound would be considered ultralight. Some poles have a built-in camera mount under the handle allowing the pole to be used as a monopod. If you are a photo buff you may want to consider this. Just remember, it adds weight.

One last thing about trekking poles. Actually, it is a request. Trekking poles typically have a carbide or steel tip. The click, click, click, click, along the Camino is dreadfully annoying. A pair of rubber tips cost just a couple of bucks. Please, make the investment and do not click. It is such a lovely gift to your fellow pilgrims to walk silently.

35

TORTILLA

My second day on my first Camino I stopped at a bar for lunch. On display was this yummy looking quiche without a crust item. Just had to try it. I asked what it was and was informed that it was a tortilla. Where I come from, California, a tortilla is altogether something else. A tortilla is made of either flour or corn, flattened and cooked in a heavy skillet. Did I not correctly hear her pronunciation of the item?

I was offered a choice of Hamon or vegetable. Vegetable please. Taking my warm "tortilla" to my table along with my coke, I discovered a potato quiche like wedge of pie. It was sort of like a thick omelet with egg and potato. It was good but nothing to swoon over.

Over the next few days, I discovered they were everywhere. You could go into any bar, café, restaurant, grocery store, roadside vendor, gas station food service area. The first one was novel. But, after a couple of days, the novelty had worn off. They are heavy, carb loaded, fill you up fast convenience food. Often, they are served in a sliced baguette as a sandwich. Wow…carb overload.

Upon returning to California, I experimented with recipes trying to come up with a "tortilla" that was more on the gourmet side of the culinary spectrum rather than the gas station fast food side. My first task was to research recipes to learn how the traditional Spanish tortillas are made. The basic recipe calls for slicing potatoes very thin, frying them in oil in a skillet until tender. Cook onion and garlic in oil until translucent. Mix eggs with seasoning in a bowl and combine everything. Put the mixture back in the skillet and cook until the eggs are set.

First of all, I had to find the best type of potato. A potato with a high starch content will fall apart when cooked. For the tortilla, the potatoes need to be layered. Therefor a potato with a low starch content will work best. Waxy potatoes are high in moisture and have a low starch content helping them keep their shape. I tried several including, red potatoes and Yukon gold. Both of these worked well but I liked the Yukon gold best.

The potatoes need to be fried in oil until tender but not brown. I do not particularly like the fried oil taste when it's overbearing so I like to use an avocado oil. It leaves a soft, rich, buttery taste which complements the fried potatoes quite nicely. Grapeseed oil is also very nice and gives a nutty taste to the potatoes. After numerous experiments, this is what I came up with. I think it's rather good. But you can be the judge.

Tortilla Española

Ingredients

- 2 or 3 Yukon Gold potatoes or similar low starch potatoes
- 6 to 8 eggs beaten
- 2 to 3 green onions chopped up to the light green parts
- ½ cup avocado oil
- Salt and Pepper to taste
- Optional herbs to try with the green onion:
  - Basil
  - red pepper flakes
  - mustard
  - paprika
  - rosemary
  - thyme

- ° oregano
- ° sage

Instructions

- Slice the potatoes using a mandolin, ¼ inch wide.
- Fry the potatoes in batches in the oil until just tender but not browned. As you remove each batch from the oil, drain on a paper towel and salt to taste.
- Sauté the green onion until just translucent. Add any other herbs as desired.
- In a cast iron skillet place the onions and herbs on the bottom, then layer potatoes in a scalloped pattern.
- Add the beaten eggs and place the skillet and shake until everything is coated. Let the mixture cook until the edges begin to set.
- Place the skillet under the broiler and cook for about 5 minutes or until the top is brown.
- Remove from the broiler and place a large dish on top of the skillet and invert. Everything is extremely hot so uses towels or potholders.
- Let it cool for a few minutes, then cut and serve. If you want to feel like you are in Spain, put it on a sliced baguette and go sit in your back yard with your boots off and feet up.

Enjoy!

36

A GARDEN OF EDIBLES

The Maseta, that large and expansive flat plain just after Burgos and ending in Astorga, is a part of the Camino Frances that pilgrims typically dread. This is because it is flat, hot, not much to see, and generates plentiful stories of blisters, heat stroke, sunburn and other not so pleasant conditions and is about 220 kilometers long. I have walked it twice and, perhaps I'm odd, but I enjoyed it both times. I enjoyed the heat. I never ran out of water. I have dark skin and don't burn easily. The lodgings along the way were wonderful, often having a pool to relax in after a long day. It was great for me. Just what I love, heat, sun, and water at the end of the day.

One afternoon, arriving in town about 3ish, I followed my normal routine of heading to the cathedral. On my way I saw an advertisement for an Albergue with a pool. Yippee!!! I'm off. The 4 dorm rooms held 4 bunk beds each so this was a small to moderate Camino accommodation. Getting situated at my assigned bed, I delayed the laundry task and opted for the pool. Ahhhhh, true bliss.

After a most enjoyable hour or so, I decided I better get back on track and tackle the laundry. The drying part of the chore would not be a problem since it was quite warm outside with a lovely breeze. Laundry complete, phone on charge, email checked, Facebook entries complete,

DR. GUYLENE GIGI TREE

time to check out dinner options. Asking Anna, the Hospitaller, about dinner options she gave me a couple of choices. After explaining to her that I prefer to eat vegetarian she got a twinkle in her eye. Anna took me out to her garden at the side of the house and gave me the grand tour.

Anna's garden was the most dazzling array of color, design, flow, accessible edibles I have ever seen. It was truly artwork. When you think of growing vegetables out in the back yard, you typically think of tomatoes or beans. This garden was remarkable which is why I'm writing about it. I learned from Anna that this type of garden is called food scaping.

Varietal baby green at the grocery store can be expensive but Anna had many plants. She explained that you can simply snip leaves from various plants whenever you wanted them. No need to pull up the whole plant. She had arugula, kale, mustard greens, and oakleaf lettuce as borders in the garden. In the herb section, she had sage, dill, parsley, basil, and rosemary. She explained that allowing some of the herb plants to go to bloom attracts pollinators that are of benefit to the overall garden.

She of course had tomatoes. But not just the typical red type. She had several varieties that climbed rose towers and up an over an arch. She had cherry tomatoes, roma tomatoes, heirloom tomatoes in various colors. I never knew there were so many different types of tomatoes.

In decorative containers she had assorted types of peppers. She explained that these plants required a lot of water, hence the containers. There were orange peppers, yellow peppers, short squat peppers, flat long peppers, hot peppers, and sweet peppers.

Then we went over to the beans. These lovely plants were trained up and along beautiful vertical structures creating a decorative trellis. She had pole beans, wax beans, snap peas, purple heirloom beans. Her favorite was the scarlet heirloom that had lovely red flowers that attracted hummingbirds.

I'm not really an eggplant lover but Anna's were gorgeous. She explained that the varietals she grew were thorn less which makes them easier to harvest. She was currently experimenting with smaller varieties in colors from white to gold to the traditional purple.

The berries were the ultimate highlight of the tour. She used the bushes as a hedge along the private entrance to her garden. She had blackberries, raspberries, golden raspberries, oh, and of course strawberries.

Now then, here is the best part of the story. She handed me a basket and told me to pick my dinner. Oh my, really? After I selected my edibles, I quickly went to the market and got a good bottle of wine, actually two bottles, some cheese and fresh bread. Anna and I sat out in the garden and enjoyed the evening. What a delightful visit we had. It was just one of those chance meetings where both parties enjoy the moment.

37

LEAVING A ROCK

There is a tradition of bringing a rock from your home, wherever that might be, and leaving it at the Cruz de Ferro. This is a symbolic act of carrying your burdens, prayers, hopes, dreams, promised commitments, and depositing them at a site as a myriad of pilgrims have done before you. The Cruz de Ferro, or Iron Cross, sits on a hill which is the highest point on the Camino Frances. Those who have partaken in this ritual typically find it to be very moving. It is a day, an hour, a moment that will be remembered with a singular understanding. I have been to the sight twice now and find it both spiritually and emotionally fulfilling.

Here is a bit of history about the site. When seen today, it is a huge pile of rocks with a five-meter wooden pole shooting straight out from the top. It is surmounted by an iron cross, a replica of the original preserved in the Museo de los Caminos in Astorga. But who put it there and why? Some historians propose that it was a landmark for the early pilgrims who traveled in the winter months. The high point on the trail with a wooden pole would be a good landmark for the pilgrims and serve as a welcoming beacon on their journey. Other historians believe that it was placed there by the Celts in pre-Christian times. It marked a spot of ritual for the travelers coming from the Celtic lands. Still others believe it may have been erected by the Romans in marking borders between territories. Regardless of who put it there or why, it has been and continues to be a special place.

Before I made my first Camino, I had read about and seen pictures and videos of the site. I wanted to place a special stone from my home. I didn't want it to be just any stone. I searched for weeks looking for that perfect nugget from my home. Once found, I needed to make it special. Armed with paints and a tiny brush, I decorated the rock with my name, home state and date of Camino, that is, Gigi – California – June 2018. Several of my close friends saw the art object I was creating and  asked if they could do one as well to send with me. Now, understand that every ounce of weight is carefully calculated. A small pebble is inconsequential. But several stones? I advised them to find something small and we would have coffee some morning and paint rocks. It was a lovely time with my friends.

The day before I would place my rock and those of my friends, I stayed the night in an Auberge in Foncebadón. This cute little village was pretty much a ghost town up until just a few years ago. As old buildings are being lovingly restored and turned into auberges, hotels, restaurants and small shops, the village deserves to be visited. The lodging I chose had a lovely private room, a pilgrim's meal in the evening and breakfast in the morning. My plan was to get up before the sun and walk to the Cruz de Ferro to watch the sunrise. The hosts of the auberge packed me a breakfast the night before which included fruit, bread, cheese, and bottled orange juice.

Getting up about 4:30 and leaving shortly after, I started the short walk of 1.9 kilometers. Lovely morning walking a quiet trail, gaining an altitude of about 100 meters. An easy stroll along the mountain path. The sky was getting lighter and the birds were twittering their morning songs to all. Then, around the bend, there it was. I could see the top of the wooden pole with the iron cross on top. My pace slowed as I took in the sight beholding the moment. Up to the base of the rock hill, take off my pack, get out my rocks, climb the hill made up of hundreds of thousands of rocks brought there by pilgrims. I sat down, leaned my back up against the wooden pole, and took it all in. What a beautiful moment. One that I will never forget.

I found the perfect location to place my stones. Said a bracha (blessing) and began the continuation of the journey. I did not see any pilgrims until my mid-day orange juice stop. What a wonderful morning.

38

GRANDSTANDS
OF PEOPLE

For a pilgrim to receive the Compostela, the certificate of completion of the Camino, the pilgrim must fulfil three basic requirements. 1) they must complete a minimum of 100 kilometers on foot or on horseback, or 200 kilometers on bicycle, 2) they must be on the Camino for spiritual or religious reasons, and 3) they must be able to validate their daily progress by getting stamps or sellos along the way.

The town of Sarria is perhaps the most well-known town on the Camino Frances. This is because it is just a little over 100 kilometers from Santiago. Thus, it is a popular place for many to begin their Camino when their goal is to just get the Compostela and they have limited time. It only takes one week to walk the distance. The Camino Frances east of this town is relatively peaceful as far as numbers of pilgrims. However, as soon as you hit this big populace, the crowds augment exponentially.

Actually, the number of pilgrims seen on the trail the previous 100 to 200 kilometers had been increasing, but it really became noticeable in Sarria. No longer could you walk into an Albergue and book a bed much less a room. One had to use the cell phone and call ahead to see if they had a bed. They do not take reservations but can tell you how many beds they have left. No longer could you walk into a restaurant and get a delightful pilgrim's meal surrounded by perhaps 8 or 10 other pilgrims. There was a waiting list you could put your name on for a table. So, while we wait, how about a glass of wine at the bar? Sorry, too many people and cannot wiggle up through the crowd. Oh my, will tomorrow morning ever come.

Next day, on the trail with a bazillion other people. Where did they all come from? My pace, not fast, but not really slow, was getting left behind by the fresh pilgrims, new boots, new packs, walking sticks click, click, click. Was that teenage girl really talking on her cell to her boyfriend? Really? Oh dear…look out. Here come the group of young German males. Oh no, it's the college kids from the east coast. My goodness but they are loud. You just want to skedaddle off the trail somewhere and hide from all this loud cacophony.

Up a small incline, around a bend, it looks like a Motor Rest Area. Some buildings, vending machines, bathrooms. And, oh my goodness, look at all those tour buses. Wow!!! Lined up like dominoes. And what is the noise? Are the tourists applauding? This is evidently a popular site along the tour route where the tourists can get off the bus and actually see a real pilgrim. We walk by to thunderous applause and don't know if we should be embarrassed or wave. How about an embarrassing wave?

— ❧ 39 ❧ —

THE THREE OPTIONS

When you apply for your Compostela, you are asked to check the box that applies to your reason for walking the Camino. The three options are 1) religious, 2) spiritual and 3) other. If you check either of the first two boxes and you walk a minimum of 100 kilometers with the necessary verifications stamps, you are eligible for the Compostela, the official document signed by the dean of the Cathedral in Santiago. It is a lovely parchment certificate written in Latin and bears the official seal, stamp, and signature with your name. If you check the box "other" you get a different document, not fancy like the official one, but nice, and it is written in Spanish.

There are a lot of reasons to walk the Camino, but you need to decide which of the three boxes to check. Here is a breakdown of the reasons with rationalizations. The easiest one to define is the "other" classification. This would include those who are walking for exercise, the challenge, an adventure, vacation, the physical goal of accomplishment, the scenery, the people, the culture, etc. There are many possible reasons, but you get the drift.

Next would be the "religious" box. This is a Christian religious pilgrimage after all. The routes all lead to the Cathedral in Santiago where the bones of Saint James are entombed. The Christian pilgrimage to Santiago de Compostela dates back over 1000 years when the relics of Saint James were discovered. It was during the reign of King Alfonso II (792-842) that the remains were taken Santiago. Eventually a cathedral was built over the site of the tomb with a community arising around the edifice. Perhaps the most time-honored reason for checking the "religious" box would be for the Plenary Indulgence, also known as the Jubilee. According to the Officina de Acogida al Peregrino (Pilgrims Office) in Santiago, "An indulgence is the full remission of all temporal punishment (time spent in purgatory) up to that point in a person's life. Individuals can gain Plenary Indulgences for themselves and also for the deceased."

The "spiritual" box is perhaps the hardest to define. This is the box I checked, and I can only offer my thoughts on this. As mentioned in previous chapters, you are alone. Only your backpack, yourself, and your thoughts. This is not an easy journey. Your days are long and often physically challenging. But, in my opinion, the greatest challenge is the emotional or spiritual aspects of being alone with the divine in whatever image you believe. The journey affords you the opportunity to strip down to your bare essence and rebuild. Those who have experienced this are probably nodding their heads and saying, "how true." Those who have not made the journey perhaps will now consider doing so. It is an amazing journey. *Baruch Hashem.*

— ❦ **40** ❦ —

GREETINGS

On the Camino when you greet other pilgrims you say "Buen Camino" or literally "Good Way." It is a simple greeting that is easy to remember and use. Regardless of your primary language, everyone uses this Spanish phrase, that is in Spain. In France and Italy, they use the same but in their language.

I remember my first time having a pilgrim speak the words to me. It was like, I was really here, on my camino. It is a nice way to greet other pilgrims as you approach them from behind preparing to overtake them on the trail. Sort of like a bicycle bell. It lets them know that you are there without scaring them at the last minute. It's a great way to begin a conversation with someone, such as "Buen Camino. Where are you from?" This type of two-minute interaction is quite common and a nice way to acknowledge or welcome your fellow pilgrims. It is amazing how many of these two-minute visit people you will see that evening in the next village.

There is another expression that is used a lot but not as frequently. It is "Ultreia!" This greeting has a history which extends far back to the early days of the earliest pilgrims. Freely translated it means something like "let's go further" or "keep going." The answering greeting is "Et suseia" or "let's go higher.

—❧ 41 ❧—

WASH AT LAVACOLLA

The village of Lavacolla is just outside of the city of Santiago. A river runs through the village and is thus called the Lavacolla River. Just imagine a group of pilgrims in medieval days journeying across Spain, almost to Santiago. The smell must have been horrendous. Here, only a short walk from the Cathedral is a lovely flowing river. What would you do? Take a bath of course, and so they did. They would cleanse their bodies and clothing preparing themselves for the last leg of the long journey, the Cathedral in Santiago. The custom remains today for pilgrims approaching the Cathedral from the east.

This custom is not unique to Santiago, or Lavacolla. It is a tradition born out of the Jewish religious community dating back to the creation story in Genesis. Hashem, G-d, brought the waters together separating them from the land. The oceans, rivers, wells, and spring-fed-lakes are all mikvahs containing waters of Divine source. Immersion in the mikveh, or ritual bath, is a customary practice for a Jewish person to achieve ritual purity. The Chabad Rabbis teach that "Immersion in the mikvah has offered a gateway to purity ever since the creation of man. The Midrash relates that after being banished from Eden, Adam sat in a river that flowed from the garden. This was an integral part of his *teshuvah* (repentance) process, of his attempt at return to his original perfection." *https://www.chabad.org/theJewishWoman/article_cdo/ aid/1541/jewish/The-Mikvah.htm*

All of the Abrahamic traditions contain some form of ritual bathing. The Jews immerse in the mikvah. The Muslims participate in the ghusl. The Christians practice the ritual of baptism. During the years of the crusades, the pilgrimage to Jerusalem and Rome, the participants would immerse themselves in a body of water prior to entering the Holy Cathedral or Temple. As Santiago became popular as a pilgrimage site, the same tradition emerged there.

Regardless of the historical implications, immersing in the Lavacolla River is wonderful after 30+ days on a Camino. After a brief swim, the pilgrim has only 10 kilometers to Santiago. Just one small hill, Monte do Gozo, then, there it is…Santiago du Compostela.

——❧ **42** ❧——

THE END OF THE EARTH

I began this book with "I was standing on a cliff overlooking the Atlantic Ocean..." and I will close this book with the same. It is not the end of the journey; it is not the end of a story. It is just the closing musical phrases of a movement in a symphony that has more to come.

Once you arrive in Santiago de Compostela, no matter how many miles you journey was, why would you want to go any further. That is the question I have often been asked by fellow pilgrims. I guess if your destination was only Santiago, then you would be justified in stopping. However, my destination has always been, and I think will always be, going all the way to that furthest point on the European continent, the End of the Earth. Not going there would be like playing 4 movements of a symphony and not playing the final coda. What is the point?

The Camino de Fisterra or Finisterre Camino is the only route that starts in Santiago de Compostela and takes pilgrims west or away from the Cathedral. The Camino travels across the lovely countryside of Galicia, about 90 kilometers to the town of Fisterra on the cape of Finisterre. From there you walk out to the lighthouse that marks the 0-kilometer point of the Camino. This, in my opinion, is the true end of the journey. How fun to dip your toes in the Atlantic Ocean.

The small fishing village of Fisterra is worthy of an overnight stay. There are a lot of hotels, refugios, alberges, restaurants, shops, beaches, water, boats. It is a lovely place. I chanced to find an outstanding restaurant that served fish just caught out of the ocean, a table overlooking the bay, an excellent bottle of wine and a seemingly endless sunset. Following a stroll along the bay, my hotel enveloped me in the sleep of total indulgence. Next morning, my last day of walking my Camino...for this year anyway.

Ulteria!

ACKNOWLEDGEMENTS

First and foremost, I would like to express my sincere appreciation and gratitude to all the wonderful volunteers at the pilgrim offices along the way, the refugios and alberges, the pilgrim welcome centers, and all those along the camino network that make the journey possible.

Mark -my husband who encouraged me to go have a good time but be safe.

Joe -my "gran ángel de nieve" ski patrol buddy and Spanish tutor.

Lisa -my friend and travel mate who gave me all those wonderfully wacky times to write about.

Tanya, Janine, and Reese -my dear friends and editors extraordinaire.

.

CPSIA information can be obtained
at www.ICGtesting.com
Printed in the USA
LVHW092336100720
660313LV00004BA/287